# Praise for *Who Do You Think You Are?*

"Here's a book so honest it won't let you off the hook. You may not realize it during the early pages but it's a book about love. Indeed, it's a story where love is redefined, and even though it traces the sometimes unbearable relationship of mother and daughter, there are insights here for all of us. And—the writing is masterly: taut, honest, and strangely satisfying."
—Frank McCourt, Pulitzer Prize–winning author of *Angela's Ashes, 'Tis,* and *Teacher Man*

"Alyse Myers candidly illuminates how challenging it sometimes is to love those closest to us, but how necessary it is to love them, if only so that we may know what love is."
—Esmeralda Santiago, author of *When I Was Puerto Rican, Almost a Woman,* and *The Turkish Lover*

"A compelling read . . . Popular memoirs are peopled now with sadists and victims, but Alyse Myers has put real people in her story. She's written a wonderful book. Completely genuine, and yet artfully done."
—Benjamin Cheever, author of *Selling Ben Cheever, The Plagiarist,* and *Strides: Running Through History with an Unlikely Athlete*

"This is a book about determination and will and ambition, the laserlike focus of a young girl driven to survive her not-so-nice Jewish family and grow up to be a different kind of parent. Her success is gratifying but bittersweet, like that of a lone climber coming back down the mountain alive. Myers

D0050485

holds back nothing in the retelling of her story, and we are with her through the whole of it—the honesty, the pain, and the hard-won love waiting for her at the journey's end. I loved this book."

—Laura Zigman, author of Animal Husbandry<br>and Piece of Work

"By the end, I felt like I'd been listening to a friend who could not lie, talking about a life she could not escape, and showing me all the wisdom she'd gained in the process of making the trip from despair to peace."

—Roland Merullo, author of The Italian Summer<br>and Golfing with God

"Alyse Myers's unflinching memoir conveys the wounds of her childhood with blunt force, tempered by reconciliation. She touches nerves central to every human life."

—Julie Salamon, author of Hospital, The Net of Dreams,<br>and The Devil's Candy

"It is still possible to write a good book about an unhappy childhood, and Alyse Myers has done just that with Who Do You Think You Are? The unself-conscious simplicity with which Myers tells her tale conceals no small amount of artfulness."

—Terry Teachout, CommentaryMagazine.com

# Who Do You Think You Are?

---

a memoir

---

ALYSE MYERS

A TOUCHSTONE BOOK
Published by Simon & Schuster
New York   London   Toronto   Sydney

This work is a memoir. It reflects the author's
present recollections of her experiences over a period of years.

TOUCHSTONE
A Division of Simon & Schuster, Inc.
1230 Avenue of the Americas
New York, NY 10020

FOR OLIVIA,
*the daughter I always hoped I would have.*


AND FOR MARC.
*My life, my love. Always for Marc.*

# PROLOGUE

I DIDN'T LIKE MY MOTHER, and I certainly didn't love her. The only time we actually had anything in common was when I had my own daughter—but by then it was too late, since my mother was to die before we really could compare notes.

I know she didn't like me either. I can't say whether she loved me, as I don't remember her ever telling me so. But her dislike was more about not understanding the monster she created, as she would say, the person who wanted so much more than she expected—or was able—to give. Or *wanted* to give. To me. To my sisters. And to herself.

My mother married my father when she was nineteen and was a widow at thirty-three. She told me that he was the only man she had ever been with, both before they married and after he died. Even when I was a child, I knew that theirs was a complicated marriage. I wanted to believe they were destined to be together, that their bitter fights had to do with his illness and her inability to cope with it. I didn't want to believe that my parents—childhood sweethearts—could end up hating each other with a passion that still frightens and saddens me to this day.

A week after her funeral in 1993, my two sisters and I were in her apartment in Queens, New York, arguing over who would get her things. I was thirty-seven and my sisters would soon be thirty-five and thirty-four. She didn't have much, and I knew we were fighting over who would get more for herself and not for who would have more of her. Who would get the ugly blue and white crystal bowl that a neighbor's daughter had given my mother after a trip to Germany as thanks for looking in on her elderly mother? Or the Lladró porcelain statue of a milkmaid that came from Spain, a gift from that same neighbor's daughter? Or the framed painting of a Moorish castle that she bought at a Greenwich Village art show and was so proud that it perfectly matched the green and gold motif of her living room?

My sisters and I took turns picking things we wanted. I forget who went first. I put my choices in one corner of the room, and I soon realized the things I chose weren't really important to me, but I wasn't willing to say so. I wasn't going to let my sisters have all of her things.

And then I remembered the box. It was the size of a shoe box, hand-carved brown wood, with a green and red skull and crossbones painted on top. It looked like a pirate's treasure chest. I don't know if my father did the painting, but I wouldn't be surprised if it had been something he made in a grade school shop class. My mother was an A student and my father barely made it through the ninth grade. I could see him doing well in shop class, though. When he showed up, that is.

I knew my father had given the box to my mother before they got married. She told me so many years earlier, when I sat on the floor watching her cleaning out her bedroom closet. Or trying to. The box sat in the middle of a pile of shoes—all colors and many missing a mate—scuffed pumps and loafers, slippers and handbags. I asked her if I could open the box, and she told me no, it was only for her. That there was nothing interesting in it and I should go back to my room.

I tried again. "When can I open it?"

"When you're older," she told me. "You're not old enough now."

I had turned thirteen the week before. That day she told me I was now officially a grown-up.

"But I'm a grown-up," I reminded her. "You told me so yourself last week."

Silence.

"When can I open it?" I repeated.

She paused. "When I'm dead," she responded. "You can have it when I'm dead. In fact, it will be my present to you."

OVER THE YEARS, whenever my mother wasn't home, I would take the box out of her closet and turn it around and around, shaking it and wondering what treasures hid inside. I wanted so much to open it, but the box was locked tight, and I couldn't figure out how to open it without breaking the lock. I once dropped it on the floor—partly by accident but partly hoping the little gold padlock would somehow spring open and whatever was inside would fall out. But the box remained shut and the top corner chipped where it hit the floor.

I looked around, afraid she would catch me, even though I knew no one was there. I knew she would kill me if she found me playing with it. So I put it back where I found it and left her room.

From that point on, I wanted to know what was inside. I knew the box was important to her. And at her apartment a few days after her death, I knew that if there was one thing I had to have of hers, it was that. That box would give me the answers to my questions: Who were my parents really? And why did my mother end up with so very little in her life?

As my sisters fought over her fifteen-year-old television set, I walked into her bedroom and over to her closet. The sliding door was off its track, as it always was when she was alive. Never a good housekeeper when my sisters and I were living with her, my mother's apartment was even more cluttered and messy after we had all moved out. Her clothes were so tightly packed in the closet that it was hard to see what was there. She never threw anything out. I could see the blue dress with the white stitching that she wore to my father's funeral twenty-six years earlier crammed next to the brown polyester slacks and the brown and white polyester blouse she wore to her chemo treatments. Her shoes were thrown in a pile on the bottom of the floor, size 7½ AAA that she always had such a hard time finding in stores. The home nurse who had taken care of her while she was dying clearly had no interest in keeping the house clean, either. What is the point? she probably had asked herself. She's going to die, anyway, so why should it matter?

I was glad I brought my largest canvas tote bag that day.

I carried it with me from room to room, knowing my sisters would think I was trying to take something they might want. I didn't care what they thought. Carrying the bag reminded me of when my mother first came to visit me and my husband in our apartment soon after we were married. She kept her handbag with her the entire time she was visiting, tightly over her shoulder, hugging it to her chest. "Ma," I said when I saw she had her bag with her in the kitchen, the dining area, the bathroom, and then back in the living room, "I promise I won't steal your money." She looked at me like I was crazy, and then I touched her bag and told her it was safe for her to leave it in one place. We both laughed, and she told me she didn't realize that she was carrying it around. I'm not sure I believed her.

Now, facing her closet, I bent over and looked on the floor and pushed aside some of her things, but I didn't see the box. I stood up, stepped back as far as I could go, jumped up a few times to see if the box was on the top shelf. I started to get nervous. I didn't want my sisters to know what I was doing. They were still looking through her things, her LP records now. I left my bag on the floor by the closet and tiptoed down the short hallway to the kitchen and to the table covered with the orange and yellow checked vinyl tablecloth with old ciga-rette burns at the place where she used to sit. Feeling like a criminal, I glanced over my shoulder a few times, hoping my sisters wouldn't notice me. I picked up one of the metal fold-ing chairs and tiptoed back to her bedroom.

I placed the chair in front of the closet, kicked off my shoes, and climbed on top. I saw the box on the shelf, hiding behind the simple blue leather pocketbook I gave her for her fiftieth birthday. I knew she would never use that bag, but I wanted her to have something that wasn't plastic and didn't have hundreds of pockets and zippers. I wasn't surprised when I saw the tag still on it. I pulled it out and shoved it into my tote bag.

Then I reached for the box, pulled it out, put it under my left arm, and climbed down from the chair, keeping my balance by grabbing onto the blue and green and white housedress she wore when playing poker with my grandparents and their friends on Saturday nights. I slipped my shoes back on and put the chair in the corner, next to her bed. There was no one now who would notice it missing from the kitchen. I slipped the box inside my bag and used my sweater to cover it. I walked out of the bedroom and saw my sisters still going through her LPs, arguing over who was going to get Barbra and who was going to get Frank.

"I'm going now," I said. "I have to get home for dinner."

"Did you take anything else?" my youngest sister barked. "You didn't take anything, did you?" I knew she would worry that I had more than she did.

"What would I take?" I asked. "There's nothing here I want."

Out in the street, I looked for a taxi to take me home to my apartment in Manhattan. After twenty minutes, I found a driver who was thrilled to go back over the Fifty-ninth Street Bridge. I leaned into the seat, lifted the sweater in the bag, and looked at the box. I thought about when I would open it. And then I thought about my mother and why our relationship was so complicated.

"Why do you want more?" she always asked me and not pleasantly. "Why is my life not good enough for you?"

I closed my eyes as the taxi went over the bridge and didn't open them until it turned the corner to my building.

When I got back to my apartment, my husband and daughter were sitting in the kitchen, laughing together and eating dinner. I was reminded how lucky I was to have my own family that was so uncomplicated. I gave my husband and daughter a kiss and then walked straight into the bedroom.

"What did you do at your mom's house?" my husband called after me. "Did you find anything special?"

"Nope," I said. "Not a thing. She didn't have a thing I wanted."

I don't know why I lied to him. I sat on the bed holding the box, tracing the outline of the skull and crossbones with my fingertip. I toyed with the lock and noticed that it would be easy to pry open. Finally, I would be able to find out what it had been hiding all of these years. All I had to do was get a screwdriver, wedge it under the metal plate, flip open the top, and all of my questions would be answered.

Instead, I walked over to my linen closet, took out a white towel, and wrapped it around the box. I opened my closet door and moved aside my shoes that were neatly stacked in white boxes. I pushed the wooden box far back into my closet, behind my shoes, and closed the door.

I can't explain why I didn't open the box that day. And I can't explain why I didn't open it until twelve years later. I don't know what I was afraid of, but all during those twelve years, I would conveniently forget it was in my closet, or when I did notice it was there, would decide I just didn't have the time to look inside.

# PART ONE

# CHAPTER 1

My mother had only one boyfriend—and she married him.

She told me that they had met in school when she was fourteen and he was fifteen. My mother was the former tomboy who lost her baby fat almost overnight, she used to tell me—the good girl from the good family with the bluest of blue eyes. I had always wanted her eyes. They were the kind of eyes everyone would notice and say, "What beautiful blue eyes you have" eyes. Her eyes changed with the light and the clothing she wore. They were a beautiful light blue when she was happy; they darkened to an angry navy when she screamed at me or my sisters or my father. She screamed a lot at my father. I couldn't understand how such beautiful eyes could have so much hate in them.

She also had the most beautiful hair. Straight and thick. Deep, rich, dark, dark brown. I used to look at old pictures of her and couldn't believe how long her hair was. She used to tell me her mother would spend hours brushing it, combing it, taking out the knots after she washed it. Pulling it and twisting it into long, snakelike curls that looked beautiful when finished but made her cry all during a process that, thankfully, happened only once a week, she told me. I couldn't believe hair that beautiful could hurt. When she met my father, she cut her hair. It was much easier to manage, she said. But it was still beautiful. My father used to tell me that he loved to run his fingers through it.

My mother also had long, beautiful fingers, but she never managed to keep her nail polish on without chipping it, and her nails were always cut short and ragged. When she went out with my father for the evening, I would watch her paint her nails with iridescent polish that looked beautiful before she left but was a chipped mess by the next morning. Her jewelry was simple: a yellow gold wedding band on her left hand and a cocktail ring—dark blue sapphires, diamonds, and rubies in a gold swirl—on the right. I don't know who bought her the cocktail ring. She never wore her engagement ring.

She wasn't a tall woman—about five feet four inches, she claimed—but I always thought she was much smaller. She never stood up straight. Her shoulders were small and narrow and slightly hunched over. I hated the way she carried herself. She always looked as if she wanted to fold herself into a corner so that no one would see that she was there. "Stand up straight," I would tell her when I was old enough to notice. "Mind your business," she would snap back.

She loved bracelets and watches, anything to show off what she thought was her most beautiful feature—her slender wrists.

Her wrists were so tiny that my sisters and I joked that she couldn't hit us hard when she went after us with a belt or a hanger because she was afraid her hands would break off.

My mother loved her mother and father, and she looked up to her older sister who wanted nothing to do with her. She did her homework and never missed a day of school. She showed me her high school notebooks once, and I was amazed by her perfect handwriting. At night, as a teen, she hung out with the girls and came home when she was supposed to. She spent her summers at a sleepaway camp in upstate New York. Her parents weren't rich—her father was an immigrant from Austria who owned a fruit stand not too far from where they lived on the Lower East Side—but they wanted her to be able to get away from the heat of the city in the summer. The fans in the apartment where my mother grew up never made the rooms cool enough.

When she graduated from high school, my mother went to work as a secretary for an importer of porcelain figurines. She said she never missed a day of work and was always happy when her boss gave her one of the samples, the ones he couldn't sell because of an imperfection only he or she could see. I still have one of those figurines. It sits in my daughter's room on a shelf so high that only my husband can reach it.

My mother's parents trusted her to do the right thing—whatever that was. And while they didn't like the fact that she was dating my father, they also knew there was little they could do about the two of them. At least while they were dating. My mother's parents didn't want my mother to marry my father. They worried that he wouldn't be able to take care of their daughter. That he wouldn't be able to keep a job.

# CHAPTER 2

MY FATHER WAS THE third youngest in a family of six—five boys and one girl. He told me he was the one his brothers and sister depended on to keep their family together.

His father had left his mother for another woman right after I was born. My mother once told me everyone knew that his mother—my grandmother—slept with men in their neighborhood to help pay her bills after he left.

Unlike my mother, whose parents worked hard to keep their family in a nice, clean building on the Lower East Side, my father grew up a few blocks away in a tenement on Cannon Street. Years later, his mother moved to a low-income housing project on the edge of New York's FDR Drive. The project was a jumble of ugly, tall brown buildings, and as a child, when we went to visit, I never could remember which building was hers. They all looked the same. It was hard for me to imagine my father living in one of these buildings. He was so handsome and he dressed so beautifully. He looked so out of place here. It didn't matter that he didn't have any money. He always looked like he did.

My mother used to tell me that he was the best-looking boy she had ever seen, and that once they were together, she never ever looked at anyone else.

He wasn't a tall man—when she wore heels, the two of them were just about the same height—but my mother told me he was the leader of the boys in the neighborhood where they grew up. He had a swagger to his walk that made him seem much taller than he was. Mickey, his friends used to call him when they were first married—after his second love, Mickey Mantle—was the one who always stood out in the crowd, my mother used to tell me. Number 7 was his number, too.

I used to listen to my father tell my mother he could have been a dental technician, compliments of the government. That if he hadn't skipped so many classes during his service in the army, he wouldn't have flunked out. But it wasn't his fault, he would tell her. The stomachaches he had then and all of his life were the reason he wasn't making more money. If he hadn't stayed in the army hospital that one day too many, he would be making real money now. He told her he complained it wasn't fair. He was sick, for chrissakes.

It didn't matter that he was sick, he was told. This is the army. They don't give you a second chance, he told her. He couldn't believe he had to leave the army with nothing more than memories of foreign places like Texas and Missouri. Can you believe it? he would ask.

Memories don't pay the bills, she would tell him.

My father worked for the post office as a clerk. I think it was my grandfather who got him the job. Your job will always be safe, my grandfather would tell him whenever he came to visit. People always had to get mail, he would say.

I know my father didn't like working at the post office. And he didn't like the fact that he was a clerk. He always felt that he was smarter than that. He told anyone who would listen that he wasn't happy that my grandfather made him work there.

I used to hear my father tell my mother that her father had no right to tell him where he should work. "He just wants to make sure we have enough money to live on," she would tell him. "When you're better, you can get a job somewhere else," she would add.

When I was seven or eight years old, my father would take me to visit his mother and youngest brother, who still lived with her in the housing project.

The best thing about those visits was that I was able to be alone with him. I always wanted to spend time with him. He wasn't home a lot. I would wake up in the morning and see that he was gone, and my mother wouldn't tell me when he was coming back. I never knew if he was going to be gone for a few hours—or a week. Or longer. Sometimes on Saturdays he would coach basketball to kids in his old neighborhood on the Lower East Side. I always hoped he would take me with him on those early Saturday mornings, but I was never invited along. I hated the boys, who were more important to him than me, but I was afraid to admit I was jealous.

So whenever he would tell me that he was going to visit his mother and that I needed to get dressed immediately if I wanted to come along, of course I got dressed right away. I loved being with him. I loved the way he looked. He always had on a new, clean sweater—wool or velour, which I loved to touch when I thought he wasn't paying attention. And he always smelled so good. Every Father's Day, my sisters and I asked my mother to buy him Canoe, the cologne he wore every day. And every day, I would sneak into the medicine cabinet in the bathroom where he kept it, and pat it behind my ears and on my wrists. I never smelled as good as he did, though.

My father was a fastidious man. His clothes were important to him. His shirts and sweaters were always folded just so in his dresser drawers. The hangers in his closet were spaced exactly the same distance apart. My mother told me he was always that way, even when she first met him. It's important, he would tell me, to dress well and take care of your clothes. People will judge you first by how you look.

My mother, on the other hand, was a slob. Her closet was stuffed with everything she ever owned, and she could never find what she needed when she needed it. She wouldn't spend a lot of money on her clothes, and that was obvious.

As soon as I was dressed, he would take my hand and lead me to the big forest green car that was always parked in front of our apartment building. He told everyone it was a Cadillac and that he got a great price on it and that it was the best car in the world and that it made him feel rich. I liked the idea of feeling rich.

I never knew how much money we had, but since my parents used to fight about money all the time, I assumed we didn't have all that much. The strange thing was that I didn't feel poor. If I needed new clothes, I got them. If I wanted to go to the movies, my mother would give me money for pop-corn and soda. We didn't go on vacations, but every summer we did go to a bungalow colony in the Catskills. It wasn't the biggest bungalow, but it was big enough for the five of us. My father drove up every Friday and stayed until late Sunday night. My mother told the other mothers that it was the least he could do for her, considering the shit hole he made her live in. Thank God for the summers, she told them. It was bad enough she had to live there the rest of the year.

He would open the car door to let me in, just like I saw in the movies. We didn't talk much on the way there. He would smoke his Parliament cigarettes—as soon as he finished one, he flicked it out of the window and lit up another—and I would play with the radio dial. I always looked forward to traf-fic on the FDR Drive during the thirty-minute trip from our apartment in Long Island City, Queens. I knew that once we got to my grandmother's house, we wouldn't stay long and that the ride home would be over in what seemed like a moment.

When we got to my grandmother's building, we would wonder together if the elevator would be working. He would press the button, and we would wait a few minutes to see if the car would come down. He would look at his watch, sigh, and then take my hand to walk me up the stairs. We would climb the seven flights and then walk toward the far end of the hall. Even if I closed my eyes, I knew I would be able to find her apartment by the smell of camphor. The odor would hit me as soon as we came up the stairs, and as we got closer to the apartment it felt like we were walking right into the round, silver metal cans with the holes that she hung in every closet in her house. No matter the season, she never opened her windows. She was afraid moths would come and eat up her clothing, she used to tell me.

My father's mother was a skinny little woman with gray hair who had a funny accent and thick green-blue veins that stuck out of her hands. My father told me she was born in Russia. I don't remember ever seeing her in street clothes. It always looked like she was wearing a nightgown. She called me "girlie" when I came to visit and patted my head hello when I came into the apartment.

I tried to remember not to wear any of my nice clothes when we went to visit, as the camphor smell would linger on me for hours afterward. I always wondered what she had that was so valuable that it had to be protected by that awful smell. My father would laugh when I asked him this. I don't remember his answering my question, though.

My father was his mother's favorite. *Everyone* knew that. He was the one she turned to for everything she needed. When she needed a little extra money, he was the one she called. I used to hear him telling people that *he* was the brother who was taking care of her. *He* was the one who loved his mother the most. The problem was he never had the money to give. At least that's what my mother would tell him.

"You gave that whore money again, didn't you?" she would scream the minute we walked in the door from my grandmother's house. "How much money did you give her this time, you fucking asshole?"

I looked up the word "whore" in the giant dictionary that sat in the library at school the first time my mother used it. After reading the definition, I turned the pages so no one would know what word I looked up.

My father would call her a bitch and tell her to shut up. That if his mother needed money to pay her rent, he didn't have to get permission to give it to her.

"How could you give her money for *her* rent, goddamn it?" my mother would scream back. "How many times do I have to ask *my* parents to pay *our* rent?"

As soon as my father and I returned from his mother's house, I would go into the bathroom, close the door, lock it, throw my clothes in the always-overstuffed hamper, and then turn on the water in the sink full force. When my sisters banged on the bathroom door telling me to come out, I would tell them I was washing my hair in the sink so it wouldn't smell like camphor. I would sit on the toilet seat listening to the rush of water, waiting for my parents to stop screaming at each other. When I heard my parents' bedroom door slam—I knew my mother would go into their room while my father would sit in the kitchen and smoke—I would come out. I always wondered why no one ever noticed that I came out of the bathroom with dry hair.

# CHAPTER 3

My mother didn't wear white at her wedding. She wore an emerald green taffeta cocktail dress with a neckline that showed off her small shoulders. She wore a matching green pillbox hat with a little green veil peeking over her forehead. My father wore a suit her parents bought for him as one of their wedding presents.

I never asked my mother why she didn't wear a traditional white wedding dress. And I never asked her why she didn't frame her wedding photo or display it on her bedroom dresser like so many of my friends' parents did. She kept all of her wedding photos in a plain white envelope that had the photographer's name printed in gold at the bottom, and she stored it in her top drawer, hidden under her slips, girdles, and panties. When she wasn't around, I would sneak into her room, take out the envelope, and look at the photographs. My parents looked so happy. She looked so beautiful. He looked so handsome.

There was a photo of my mother's parents at the wedding in the envelope as well. They didn't look as happy as the bride and groom.

In 1958, two years after I was born, my parents moved from their one-room apartment near her parents on the Lower East Side to an apartment in a housing project in Long Island City, a few minutes from the Fifty-ninth Street Bridge. My parents moved there after my mother's father insisted that the two of them live someplace they could afford. Long Island City was that place.

A few months after we moved there, my middle sister was born, and her crib sat next to my parents' bed. I slept in a small bed in the room next to theirs.

I remember asking my mother when my sister was going back home. This *is* her home, my mother would tell me, annoyed. She's your sister and you should love her, she would tell me. Eleven months later, my youngest sister was born. My middle sister and her crib moved into my room, and the new baby slept in a carriage next to my parents' bed.

The summer before I started kindergarten, my mother would take the three of us downstairs each day to sit with all of the other mothers on the green wooden benches in front of our building as soon as she finished her morning coffee. There was a long row of dark blue carriages, one after the next, and the mothers would scream at all of the kids not to go into the street and to stay right here, and to wait till your father gets home, while rocking the carriages back and forth.

On most days, my youngest sister would sleep in the carriage and my mother would hold my middle sister on her lap while she talked to the other mothers. My middle sister would suck on her bottle or chew on the animal crackers my mother would feed her one by one. I would sit on the bench next to my mother, playing with a small brown bear my father bought me on one of his trips or drawing with my Crayola crayons in my coloring books. My mother would always tell everyone how lucky she was that this one was so easy, pointing to my middle sister, and that the baby was, too, thank God. Not like the big one, she would tell everyone, looking at me.

"Thank God," she would repeat, "especially as this one was a big surprise," pointing to my youngest sister in the carriage.

I always thought surprises were good things and couldn't imagine why anyone would think that my youngest sister was something good.

One morning, we got to our bench a little later than usual. It had rained earlier that day and we waited for it to stop and for the sun to come out. My mother wiped the bench with a wad of paper napkins she had stuffed in her pocketbook before we left the apartment. She tossed the wet napkins into the metal garbage can that stood right next to the bench.

While she was talking to one of the other mothers, I slid off the bench and walked a few feet to the low chain-link fence, next to the building's entrance, that separated the dirt and grass from the concrete sidewalk. My mother warned me to stay away from the dirt. I sat on the chain fence, swinging back and forth, back and forth, back and forth, until I fell backward into the wet dirt. I didn't hurt myself, as the fence was low, and I tried to get up fast so my mother wouldn't see that I fell. I could feel that the back of my sweater was wet, and my hands got covered with mud when I tried to break my fall. I tried to clean myself off before she noticed, but at that moment she turned and saw me struggling to get the dirt off. She stood up, holding my sleeping middle sister in front of her, around her waist, and ran the few steps to me. The animal cracker box fell to the ground. My middle sister started to cry.

"Shhh, shhhh, shhhh," she hushed her. She bent over and picked up the cracker box. She struggled to open the box with one hand while she held my sister. She finally managed to get a cookie out of the box and put it in my sister's mouth. The box fell to the ground again. My sister stopped crying as she sucked on the cookie.

"You stupid idiot," she hissed at me, grabbing my wrist with her hand. "I told you not to play in the dirt." Still holding on to my wrist, she walked over to the garbage can where she had thrown out the wet napkins earlier. She dropped my wrist, reached in to get the napkins, and then started wiping my dirty fingers. I could feel myself starting to cry.

"Don't you cry," she snarled as she kept wiping my fingers. "And don't you wake up your little sister."

By then, the other mothers were quiet. My mother tossed the wet napkins back into the garbage can and told me we were going upstairs and for me to shut up.

"Hold on to the carriage handle," she demanded, grabbing my wrist, putting it on the silver metal bar. With her foot she unlocked the carriage brake and pushed the carriage with one hand.

When we got to our floor, she told me to wait by the door until she could get a washcloth to clean my hands and not to touch anything. As I walked in front of her, she saw that the back of my sweater was caked with mud, too.

"I just did a wash yesterday," she whispered through her teeth. It wasn't a nice whisper. I could tell she wanted to scream at me, but she didn't want to wake my youngest sister, still asleep in the carriage. "Do you think I have nothing else to do but to wash your goddamn sweater again? I told you not to get it dirty."

I didn't say anything. I waited while she unlocked the door. She pushed it open, held the door, and told me to go right to the kitchen and wait. To not touch anything. To. Just. Wait. I walked the few steps to the kitchen. She took the handle of the carriage with one hand and pushed it into our apartment and closed the door. She carried my middle sister into the bedroom and left my still-sleeping youngest sister in the carriage.

She marched over to the sink, plugged the drain, and turned on the faucet. As the water rushed into the sink, she told me to take off my sweater and undershirt NOW, to hand them to her NOW, to get on the plastic stepstool that sat on the floor next to the sink NOW, and then to put my dirty hands in the sink as soon as the water was filled halfway. She said she was going to get the Ivory soap from the bathroom.

And that she would be back in a minute. She hurried off down the hallway.

I watched the water get high and higher. As soon as it reached what looked like the halfway mark, I bent over and dipped my hands into the sink, just like she said.

The water was scalding hot and I shrieked. I pulled my hands out of the sink and tried to stuff them into my mouth. She ran back into the kitchen, and as soon as she realized what had happened, moved over to the refrigerator, opened the freezer door, and pulled out the ice trays. I kept crying. Louder and louder. By this time, my youngest sister had woken up and you could hear my middle sister crying now, too. My mother kept saying she was sorry, she was so sorry, and to stop crying, and that she was sorry. She banged the ice trays on the counter, put the ice into the red and white checked dish towel that hung on the wall next to the sink, pulled my hands out of my mouth, held them together, and then wrapped the towel around them.

A neighbor from down the hall rang the doorbell to see what was going on and to ask if my mother needed any help.

"Just a little accident," my mother told her when she opened the door, peeking through the chain lock. "Everything is okay. This is what happens when you have three kids and they all wake up at the same time," I heard her say. "I'll take care of it from here."

Soon we were all quiet.

My mother picked me up and carried me into her bedroom—my hands still wrapped with the towel—and put me on their bed. I closed my eyes and went to sleep.

As soon as I heard my father's key in the door, I got up, ran down the hall to the door, and grabbed his leg and cried. My mother told him what happened, how I put my hands in hot water by accident and how sorry she was. She told him I had been making her crazy and that she couldn't believe she had made such a mistake.

"How could you do that?" he yelled at her. "How could you not know the water was hot? Do you want to be arrested? How could you do that to a child?"

He picked me up and carried me back into their bedroom. I put my head on his shoulder. When we got to their bed, he moved the covers aside, stacked the two pillows on top of each other, and leaned me against them. He sat down next to me. Then he opened the towel and looked at my hands.

He bent over and kissed my fingers, one by one. And then my palms. And then the backs of my hands.

"You're fine now," he said. "All better."

He put the covers over me and told me to go to sleep and have sweet dreams.

And then he left.

# CHAPTER 4

As I GOT OLDER, I dreamed of having my own room and not having to share it with my sisters. I wished I were an only child. I hated sharing my room with the two of them. When my youngest sister was too big for the carriage, she moved into the crib. My middle sister moved into a small bed. Soon, three small beds were squeezed into the tiny room. And then when I was eight years old and my sisters were six and five, my parents bought a bunk bed for me and my middle sister so the room wouldn't be so crowded.

I loved the bunk bed. I had the top. I used to look out the window from my perch and pretend I was a princess who was one day going to live in a beautiful apartment with a room just for me. Whenever my middle sister would kick my mattress from her bed below, I would dream about living in a new building, a building where I wouldn't be afraid the elevator would get stuck and we wouldn't smell the incinerator.

There was a huge smokestack next to our building that blew black sooty pieces through our windows no matter the season. In the winter, our windows were wide open because the radiators were burning hot, and in the summer they were open because we didn't have air conditioners. During the summer, my sisters and I took turns taking a cool bath each night before we went to bed. As soon as we each finished, we ran out of the bathroom wrapped in a towel, racing to get to our room before our mother yelled at us for dripping water on the floor, and then lay on our beds, still damp, fanning ourselves with our hands to get a breeze—any kind of breeze. Our building sat on Twenty-first Street, one of the noisiest and busiest streets in the neighborhood, facing a garage where garbage trucks were stored and went in and out at all hours.

When people came to visit us, they always asked how we could live there with so much noise. What noise? we would answer, surprised. We had become so used to it that the noise was part of our daily rhythm.

I never wanted my friends to visit me. It didn't matter if they lived in our building or across the street. I wasn't proud of my apartment, and I never knew if my parents were going to be fighting. My parents never seemed to notice—or care—that someone from outside our immediate family might witness their unhappiness. I didn't want my friends to know about the fighting in my house. I was always afraid my father was going to do something or say something that would set my mother off—usually about why he hadn't come home or how much money he spent—and then the two of them would go at it. She used to yell at him a lot about how much money he spent on himself.

"It's your fault we live in this shit hole," she would scream at him. "If you had a good job and you didn't spend all of your money on your clothes, we could get the hell out of this place. I'm sick of smelling everyone else's pee in the halls.

"I hate your fucking guts," she would add.

He would tell her to drop dead. And tell her to ask her mother for money. And then he would leave. And then we wouldn't see him for days.

I USED TO WONDER how two such good-looking people could be so ugly to each other.

I couldn't understand how two people who seemed to love each other one day could hate each other the next. Sometimes in the morning, I would sneak into their bedroom and see my father's leg over my mother's body, his leg hugging her side while the two of them were oh-so-close that they seemed to be attached. I grew up wanting a man to possess me that same way. Then later that day their bodies would be tight with anger and they looked like two strangers during a fight. My sisters and I would cry for them to stop screaming at each other during those fights.

One day, I overhead my next-door neighbor tell another neighbor she couldn't wait for the screamers to move out of the building. I saw her point at me. Then, she said, she might actually be able to get a good night's sleep.

My parents must have been happy when they were first married, I used to think. At least I wanted to believe that to be the case.

They looked so good together. I used to think I was lucky that I had such attractive, young parents. My mother was almost twenty-three years old when she had me, and my father was almost twenty-four. They were the youngest of all of the parents in my school, and I was so proud of that. So many of my friends' mothers and fathers looked old and fat or had funny accents. Not mine. I always hoped my parents would come to my school together so I could show them off to my friends and teachers.

But they never did.

I don't remember my father going to any of my school conferences, as he was often in the hospital. Something about his stomach, my mother would say, waving me off when I tried to ask her why he wouldn't be coming. Again. But when he signed my report cards, he would also write notes telling my teachers how much he appreciated their work. My teachers would always tell me how lucky I was to have such a good father.

When I finished third grade, in 1965, he wrote me this note:

*To my daughter:*

> *There are parents who are constantly complaining about how much they do and give to their children. I have already received from you much more than I can ever hope to give.*
>
> *Love, Daddy*

I loved him so much. I loved that he would tell me how pretty I was and how smart I was. I loved that he would tell me I was going to be someone important when I grew up. I hated that my mother didn't love him as much as I did. Why did she scream at him all the time? I wondered. He would tell her he was going to live his life the way he wanted. That he was going to come and go as he pleased. If he wanted to go to work, he would. If he didn't feel like going in, he had plenty of sick days. That's why he worked for the post office, he would remind my mother when she worried that he would get fired for staying out for so long. He had the right to do anything he wanted, he would tell her. And to see anyone he wanted. If she didn't like it, she could go complain to her goddamn parents.

All I knew was that I had a father who would disappear for a while—sometimes weeks at a time, sometime months—and then come back with new clothes for him and some kind of gift for me and my sisters. A little trinket—a key chain with the Liberty Bell from Philadelphia, a gold shoehorn from Washington, D.C., a red plastic Beatles wallet. It didn't matter what it was. I was so happy he was home.

# CHAPTER 5

When my mother and father got married, my mother told me the first thing my father asked her to cook for him was bacon. Both my parents were Jewish. My father's family was observant; my mother's was not.

We were one of only two Jewish families in the building, and there were very few Jews in our housing project. It seemed there were very few Jews in Long Island City at the time. Most of my friends were Irish or Italian. We got a present every night of the eight days of Hanukkah because my father wanted to convince us *ours* was the better holiday.

"*They* only have *one* day," he would tell my sisters and me as we watched him twist that night's orange bulb into the beige plastic menorah he kept displayed on the windowsill plugged in from the moment the holiday began until the end. "We have *eight*."

And then he would hand us each that night's present.

One year, my youngest sister got the Skipper doll she had begged my mother to buy as soon as she saw it advertised on television. My middle sister and I preferred Barbie, but she wanted Barbie's younger sister with the bright red-orange hair. The next day, I convinced my youngest sister that her doll should have the same haircut she had—a pixie. Now you look alike, I told her when I finished cutting off most of the doll's hair. You look just like twins.

"How could you ruin your sister's doll?" my mother said later, when my sister showed her what I had done. "Why didn't you cut your own doll's hair?"

"She said I could," I told my mother. "Didn't you?" I demanded.

"You made me," she whined. "You made me."

"You said I could cut it!" I reminded her. "Didn't she?" I asked my middle sister. "Didn't she?"

"You made her," my middle sister said. "And you told her it would grow back."

The next week, my mother took me to the neighborhood beauty parlor and told the hairdresser my hair was too unruly and to give me a trim. To make it easier to handle, she told him. I didn't say a word while I watched him cut my long curly hair into a short, short haircut.

"Do you like it?" the hairdresser said when he finished.

I didn't look like me anymore.

I nodded, turning my face away from the mirror. I couldn't look.

As soon as I got outside the shop, I started to cry.

"Now you'll know how it feels," my mother said.

THE SYNAGOGUE CLOSEST to our apartment building was an Orthodox one, and my parents decided I would attend Hebrew school there. I got the news one evening as I was sitting at the kitchen table doing my homework.

It was the third week of school. I had just begun the third grade. My father was at the table finishing his dinner while reading the sports pages of the *New York Post*.

My mother sat in her chair—the one closest to the kitchen—and told me that she had signed me up for Hebrew school and that it was starting next week. I was expected to go to class in the afternoon right after regular school. She told me that I was also expected to go to synagogue on Friday nights and Saturday mornings. Oh, and that I wouldn't be able to be a Brownie after all since I wouldn't be able to attend the meetings now, with Hebrew school, and that I would have to give back my Brownie uniform, too.

I had dreamed of becoming a Brownie since I was in kindergarten and was so excited when I finally got the chocolate brown uniform the second day of school. All of my nine-year-old friends in the third grade were part of the troop, and we loved walking the halls wearing our uniforms and brown headbands on the afternoons we had a meeting. I couldn't wait to do all of the fun things I had heard we would do, like make Christmas tree ornaments and decorate Easter eggs.

I begged my mother to reconsider.

I'll go to Hebrew school when I'm in fifth grade, I promised. Please just let me be a Brownie now. I *have* to be a Brownie, I told her. I just *have* to.

She shook her head.

"I'm not going," I told her. "You can't make me."

"It's really not up to you," she told me. "I said you're going, so you're going."

I looked at my father. He hadn't looked up from his paper.

"I'm not going," I told her again. "I don't want to go to Hebrew school."

I looked at my father again. I couldn't believe he wasn't saying anything.

She told me I was Jewish and that I was going, and that there was going to be no more discussion and that I should shut up and stop fighting with her and to get the hell away from the table and to go to my room. Or else.

I didn't want to find out what the "or else" meant. But I couldn't let her have the last word.

But we're not really Jewish, I told her. We eat bacon, I reminded her.

She stood up so fast the chair tipped over backward. She leaned over to me and grabbed my notebook.

"Did you hear what I said?" she hissed. "Get out," she said. "Get out of here now."

She flung my notebook across the table and it fell on the floor.

"Get out," she said again. "Now."

I knew that if I didn't get out of her way, she would hit me. Hard.

I gathered up my books, left the table, and went straight into my room. My middle sister, who was seven at the time, asked me what the screaming was all about. I ignored her. She was sitting on her bed, brushing her long, stringy hair. The hair my mother was always telling her to keep out of her eyes. My youngest sister, who was six years old, was sitting on the floor playing with her Skipper doll, the doll whose hair I had cut short.

I reached into my closet and took the uniform off the hanger. My middle sister stopped brushing her hair and asked me why I was putting on that stupid uniform and I told her it didn't matter and to mind her own business. You look really ugly in brown, she told me. My youngest sister started to laugh and she said I looked really ugly in brown, too. I turned my back on the two of them, finished buttoning the front, and then walked to the bathroom and closed the door. I jumped up a few times to try to see my whole image in the mirror over the sink. I opened the door, went back into my room, took off the uniform, folded it up, and then went into my parents' room. I left the folded uniform on the bed on my mother's side. I put the headband in my pocket and walked back into my room.

My father stopped by the door. "Don't be upset," he told me. "Listen to your mother. Be a good girl and listen to your mother."

I turned away.

"You'll like Hebrew school," he continued. "It will be good for you to learn about your religion. Especially in this neighborhood."

I still wouldn't look at him.

"When did you cut your hair?" he added.

I wanted to ask him why he wouldn't help me. Why he let my mother be so mean to me. And why he was never around to protect me. But I didn't. He went into his room and closed his door.

THE FOLLOWING WEEK, I started Hebrew school. And I found that I liked it and actually looked forward to going each day. Of course I wouldn't admit this to either one of my parents. Especially my mother.

As soon as regular school finished at three o'clock, I would grab my books and run the two blocks to the synagogue. I decided I really didn't care about being a Brownie and didn't pay attention when my friends told me about all of the things they were doing.

Sometimes when I came home to our apartment building, I would see a girl, another nine-year-old who lived there, waiting for me. She was one of the girls in the Brownie troop, and I always regretted telling her I had to quit because of Hebrew school.

"Jew girl," she would taunt when she would see me. "Stupid Jew girl." Sometimes she would stick out her foot and try to trip me.

She was much bigger than me, and I was afraid of her. And I was afraid to tell anyone about her. I didn't want to admit I couldn't fight back.

Every day I would pray she wouldn't be there and that she and her family would move away.

One afternoon, my father found me sitting outside our apartment door, crying. I didn't want to go inside and let anyone see that I was upset. I finally told him what had been happening, and I begged him to move us to another building. Or at least hit her so hard she would never bother me again. He laughed and told me he couldn't do that. And that we would move one day to a big house but in the meantime he had the perfect solution and he would give it to me the next day. He took my hand and we went into our apartment. I wondered all night what he was going to do.

The next day, I was thrilled when I didn't see her waiting for me. I assumed my father had done what he had promised. I told myself I knew he wouldn't let me down.

That next evening, he came home from work and handed me a red leather diary with a shiny gold lock and key.

Here's how you'll get her back, he told me. I looked at him, not understanding how that diary would help me.

Write it down, he said. Write it down. Anytime you have a fight with someone, you write it down and you'll feel better.

# CHAPTER 6

THE WEEKS MOVED BY quickly that fall. I was busy with third grade and Hebrew school—and homework for both. I didn't have time to notice that my father wasn't around again. I didn't ask my mother where he went or when he was coming back. I knew she wouldn't tell me. Sometimes I wondered if she even knew.

And as much as I missed my father, I had to admit the house was a lot quieter when he wasn't around. And my mother was a little nicer.

Every Tuesday at five o'clock, after Hebrew school, I would meet my mother and sisters at the pizza place with the red and green striped awning two blocks away from the syna-gogue. My father never joined us. I assumed he had to work late at the post office, making sure the mail would be deliv-ered the next day. My mother would remind us she deserved to go out once a week to eat and not have to cook.

I liked it better when my father didn't come to dinner with us. I liked it better when he and my mother weren't together in a restaurant.

When we were younger, the five of us would go out to eat every Sunday night at the neighborhood Chinese restaurant. My sisters and I would sit on one side of the big red booth and my mother and father would sit on the other side.

My mother would order an apricot sour as soon as the waiter handed us the menus. As soon as the drink came, my sisters and I would fight over who would get the bright red maraschino cherry that decorated her drink. I can't remember what my father ordered.

Between bites of egg rolls, wonton soup, spare ribs, and roast pork lo mein, the two of them would take turns lighting each other's cigarettes, stopping their smoking only at the end of the meal, when the waiter would toss fortune cookies on the table when he brought the check.

My mother would grab a cookie, break it open, and read her fortune.

"You will have a happy life," she read one night, slurring her words.

My father took his cookie, cracked it open, and pulled out the skinny white strip of paper. "You will make a lot of money," he read aloud.

"I like mine better than yours," he told her. And then he lit up another cigarette.

"You're an asshole," she said. And then she blew smoke in his face.

I liked going to the pizza place better since my mother smoked only when she finished her last slice.

On one of those Tuesdays, in November, a little after the four of us sat down in our usual booth and started to eat our slices, the lights started to flicker. We looked at each other— and then continued eating. Other than the counterman, we were the only ones in the pizza place at that hour. I didn't have any friends who went out to dinner during the week.

The lights continued to flicker and then went out. The pizza man laughed about not paying his bill. We sat in the dark and waited. And waited. It didn't seem like the lights would go on again soon. My mother told us to stay at the table and she walked over to the door and looked outside. My youngest sister started to follow her.

"Sit," she said. "Don't move. Finish your pizza."

She stood by the door and then came right back and sat down. I got up and walked over to the door. I was surprised she didn't yell at me to sit down. All of the streetlights were out. I started to worry about how we were going to get home.

I asked my mother if she knew where my father was. She said she had no idea and pulled out a cigarette. She handed one to the counterman. The smell of smoke and cheese and tomato sauce made me feel sick.

A policeman came into the pizza place. He told us the en-tire city was covered in darkness. My youngest sister started to cry and asked if we were all going to die. My mother told her to shut up and finish her slice.

My mother paid the counterman and we walked back to our apartment building in the dark. It was strange to see all of the buildings without any lights in the windows. There were so many people in the street. It was a cool, crisp evening, and I wasn't dressed warmly enough. I had forgotten my light blue scarf at Hebrew school and I wished I had taken it with me.

When we got to our building, most of our neighbors were outside talking about what had happened and where they were when the lights went out. It was getting chilly. Finally, one of our neighbors led us up the four flights of stairs with his flashlight. He asked when my father would be home, and my mother told him she was sure it would be soon. I asked my mother if she knew where my father was and how he would get home. She didn't answer. The neighbor held the flashlight and waited while the four of us entered the apartment and then sat together at the kitchen table.

My mother leaned over and turned on the transistor radio that always sat on the windowsill next to her chair, and the radio told us over and over again of the people trapped in subways under the city and in elevators.

Then she reached into her bag, pulled out her cigarette pack, and started smoking. She finished one, ground it into the ashtray, picked up the lighter she threw on the table after she lit the last one, and started all over. I wondered how many more cigarettes before the lighter wouldn't work anymore. Every time she lit another one I felt myself jump a little bit when I heard the lighter flicking against her finger. I was afraid she was going to burn her finger with the lighter. She didn't look at us—she just looked out the window, and as I looked at the side of her face, I watched the ashes at the end of the cigarette glow reddish orange each time she inhaled. She held the smoke in her mouth for a long time. The four of us sat at the table saying nothing. It was so dark in the house.

All of a sudden she got up from her chair, and we watched her try to pull the window shade up all the way with one hand. It wouldn't go up, so she tugged at it with both hands, pulling it down and then trying to push it up, with the cigarette hanging out of her mouth. I hoped the ashes wouldn't fall and start a fire. Finally, she got the shade to go all the way up, and she sat back down. I was glad there was a moon in the sky that evening and that there was now a little more light in the apartment.

My youngest sister asked what would happen if my father never came home. My mother turned her head and told her to shut up. Then she said it was time for us to go to bed. She got up and led the way to our bedroom. It was the first time my mother didn't make us wash up before we went to sleep. As soon as we were in our beds, my youngest sister begged my mother not to close the door.

"You'll be fine," my mother said. "Just go to sleep." She closed the door halfway.

The three of us lay in our beds trying to fall asleep.

"Is Daddy ever going to come home?" my youngest sister asked us both.

"Of course he will," I said. "Of course he will."

❧

EARLY THE NEXT morning, my father came into the apartment singing.

I had just woken up and I could hear his key going into the lock. I ran into the hallway as soon as he got in the door.

He was carrying his *New York Post*.

My mother was sitting at the table. She was wearing the same clothes she had on at the pizza place the night before. Smoking. The lights weren't on and the shade was still up.

My father flicked the switch for the overhead light. He tossed the paper on the table. I remember the word "Why?" was in big letters on the front page. Right under the word "blackout."

"Why?" was a good question, I thought. About a lot of things.

"You're home," I said. "You're home."

He kissed me on the cheek.

"Where were you?" my mother hissed at him. "I've been waiting all night for you to come home."

He didn't answer her.

"How could you leave us alone and not call me, you bastard?" she said to him.

He just looked at her. I waited for him to say something. We were so worried about him and I wanted to tell him that.

"Answer me," she screamed at him. "Answer me, you selfish son of a bitch. How could you not call me and let me know where you were? How could you not call to make sure we were okay? And don't tell me you couldn't find a phone we were okay? And don't tell me you couldn't find a phone that worked, you bastard. Don't you care about us, you piece of shit?"

She sounded like she was out of breath. Her eyes were red and watery.

"Don't you care about us?" she repeated. But this time she was whispering. It was almost as if she was talking to herself.

I started to wonder if she was right. Didn't he care about us?

Finally, he answered. "What's the big deal?" he said. "I'm home now."

# CHAPTER 7

BUT NOT FOR long.

A few days after what became known as the Great Northeast Blackout of 1965, he told me he was going away for a while and to be good while he was gone. I tried to forget about that morning.

He would be home soon, he promised. I had gotten used to him disappearing and not telling me. This was the first time he made a point of letting me know he was going to be away. I wanted to tell him not to leave but I knew it wouldn't make a difference. So I didn't say anything.

But every day, after he left, I would ask my mother when he was coming back home, and she would say, "Soon."

"But when?" I would insist. "Tell me when."

"I said soon," she would say. "Stop asking me, for god-sakes."

"But why don't you know?" I would push.

She would turn away.

I knew that was my cue to stop asking. But I couldn't help myself. I wanted him to come home.

"But why?" I called after her.

She turned and raised her hand at me. "If you ask me one more time I'll get the strap," she said.

I stopped asking.

SOMETIMES WHEN THE PHONE RANG I would rush to answer it to see if it was him.

It never was.

At night, I would stay up as long as I could, hoping to hear his key turn in the lock. I kept my transistor radio next to me, singing to myself to stay awake.

I loved my radio. It sat in a tan leather case that I never removed. As soon as I got into bed I would take it out from under my pillow, put it next to my ear, and turn it on. My father had given it to me when he came back from one of his trips. Every morning I put it back under my pillow so that it was there for me later that night. Often I fell asleep with it on.

In the morning, I would sneak into my mother's room to see if he had come home while I was asleep. I could see his side hadn't been touched.

I don't know why this time it mattered so much to me. But

it did. I wanted him back. The blackout scared me and made me worry that really bad things could happen when our family was apart. I wished I had someone to talk to. And even if I did, I knew I wouldn't admit that I was afraid. And I didn't want my mother to hit me with the strap.

I don't remember my sisters ever asking about him. Maybe they were too young to notice, I told myself, as I counted the days for him to come back. And then I would fall asleep.

*Ding-dong ding-dong ding-dong.*

He was back.

And they were fighting again.

*Ding-dong ding-dong ding-dong.*

It was late in the night and he was ringing the doorbell. He wouldn't stop.

I could tell this wasn't the usual I-hate-you-and-wish-you-were-dead fighting.

It was the kind of fighting even a ten-year-old knows means the end.

The radio was playing quietly next to my ear, on my pillow. Paul McCartney was singing "We Can Work It Out" to me.

> *Try to see it my way*
> *Do I have to keep on talking till I can't go on?*

*Ding-dong ding-dong ding-dong.*

I pressed the radio even closer to my ear. I wanted the radio to help drown out the sounds of a marriage falling apart. This was not the first time this had happened when he came home after one of his absences. I sometimes fell asleep in school after those nights when I stayed up late trying not to listen to their fighting—and stayed awake listening only to the radio.

> *When a man loves a woman*
> *Can't keep his mind on nothing else*

I turned the volume up a little louder. Not too loud so that I would wake my sisters. But loud enough so that the only thing I told myself I could hear was Percy Sledge singing about the woman he loves.

*Ding-dong ding-dong ding-dong.*

I heard the door push hard against the chain lock.

"Open the door," he screamed.

"Go back to your girlfriend," she screamed back.

I pretended I didn't hear her say that. I hugged the radio even more tightly to my ear. I could feel the back of my pearl earring sticking into my skin. It hurt but I decided to ignore the pain.

I don't like Frank Sinatra. He reminded me of my parents when they used to drink too much and then dance to one of his albums, usually *Strangers in the Night,* on the record player in our living room.

My sisters and I would hear the music, and sometimes the three of us would sneak out of our bedroom, wearing our matching pink one-piece pajamas with feet and shushing each other so my parents wouldn't know we were there. We would hide behind the bookcase that separated the living room from the hallway and watch them.

I don't think my parents had any idea that we were watching them, and even if they did, I'm not sure they would have cared.

My sisters would get bored and go back to our room. I stayed.

I watched my mother, with her glassy eyes, laugh too loudly at my father while he would half twirl her. Sometimes she would stumble and he would try to catch her before she fell. She would grab at his shirt, his pants, his belt—anything to stop her from falling. And when she did fall, he would try to pick her up while the two of them were laughing and singing to the music. Sometimes you could see she couldn't get up and he would get on the rug, too, and put his body on top of hers.

"Get off me," she would tell him. "Get your fucking hands off me."

She would hit him, pounding her fists against his chest. It didn't look like she was hurting him and I was glad. Still lying over her, he would lean back, grab her wrists, and push her hands down on the floor. He would start to kiss her face, her neck, and then he would push his body even closer to hers. She never closed her eyes. I would watch her stare at him.

And then she would start to laugh.

"Get up, asshole," she would tell him. "Get me up."

He would get up and grab her hand and make her stand up and they would finish their dance.

I didn't like seeing them that way. I didn't recognize these people who called themselves my "parents."

You could tell our living room was too small for the kind

of dancing they wanted to do, but it didn't seem to matter to them. They listened so carefully to the music you could see they could see or hear nothing else.

I would hear this line over and over:

*Lovers at first sight, in love forever.*

And then they would look into each other's eyes and sing together:

*"For strangers in the night."*

My mother used to joke that when she was in school, her teachers told her not to sing, just to mouth the words of songs during assembly. That's how bad her voice was. I could understand why her teachers would tell her that. My father didn't seem to notice, though.

*Dingdongdingdongdingdongdingdong.* The bell was as angry as he was.

"Open the goddamn door." He was ringing the bell and pounding on the door at the same time.

"Open it," I whispered to myself. "Please just open it."

"Tell your girlfriend to open her fucking door," she screamed back. "What's the matter? Your girlfriend, she doesn't want you?"

And then I heard silence. The bell stopped ringing long enough for me to believe it wouldn't ring again that evening. I realized I'd been holding my breath, and I let the air out slowly.

I heard my mother bolt the top lock. Click.

And then the bottom lock. Click.

I could hear her walking to her bedroom. She closed her door.

I listened to my sisters breathing quietly. I wondered if they were having sweet dreams.

I turned off the radio and closed my eyes.

# CHAPTER 8

I DIDN'T KNOW THAT it was called a colostomy. All I knew was that my father had an ugly, bright red, open sore on his stomach that made me feel sick every time I thought about it.

I saw it by accident. I must have been ten years old at the time. My father hadn't closed the door to the bathroom all the way—we had only one bathroom in our apartment for the five of us—and I rushed in one day after I had been playing outside. I was holding myself I had to go so badly. I pushed open the door and was shocked to see my father sitting on the toilet with this ugly red thing sticking out of his stomach.

"Get out," he screamed at me. I had never seen him so angry with me.

He didn't have to tell me twice. I flew out of the bathroom so fast I forgot I had to go. I went to my room and turned on the radio. I decided I would try to forget what I saw. After what seemed like hours, I peeked out of my room and saw the bathroom door open. It was safe to go in. I went quickly, trying not to notice the sticky sweet smell that lingered after my father used the bathroom. I never understood where that smell came from.

Later I asked my mother what was on my father's stomach.

"It's how he goes to the bathroom," she said.

I didn't understand.

"He had an operation," she told me. "He goes to the bathroom in a bag."

I still didn't understand but decided I didn't want to ask any more questions.

One day all five of us were going to visit my mother's parents. We were by the front door of our apartment, just about to leave. My father had his keys out, ready to lock the door. He paused, handed the keys to my mother, and told her he needed to go to the bathroom one more time. He would be back in a second. Promise.

She took the keys and didn't say a word. He opened the door and closed it behind him. Quietly. She didn't look at us and we didn't look at her. We waited. It was getting hot in the hallway. I was wearing a navy blue turtleneck sweater that was starting to feel itchy against my neck.

I could smell a neighbor's cooking. Eggs and onions

filled the hallway. I put my nose into my sweater, holding my breath, trying to breathe in the smell of the wool and the soap I washed my face with earlier. I was afraid I was going to throw up.

We waited.

And waited.

And then my mother shoved the keys into my hand. She said something under her breath but I couldn't understand what she said. I didn't want to understand what she said. She grabbed the knob of the door, turned it, and pushed it open. As it came back toward me, I put my knee against it so it wouldn't slam. My sisters looked at me but said nothing.

I could hear her heels move down the hallway to the bathroom. It wasn't a long hall.

She banged on the bathroom door and told him to GET. OUT. NOW. That he was taking too long, that he should open the door. NOW. I could hear her twisting the doorknob back and forth and back and forth while she was banging on the door.

"Open the door," she screamed.

"In a minute," he screamed back.

I held the apartment door with my knee. My sisters and I knew not to move. This was not the first time this had happened.

Whenever we would go out as a family, we would wait and wait and wait for my father to be ready. My mother, on the other hand, would put on a streak of bright red lipstick, take a comb through her hair, and be ready to go.

My father would cry that he couldn't get the tape that was

supposed to attach his bag to him to stick properly. He would cry and curse at the same time.

That day in the hallway, my mother didn't care. She wanted him to hurry up.

He deserved it, she told him.

"What's the matter? You can't go, you bastard? Ask your girlfriend to help you go. Want me to help you go? I'll stick a hanger up your ass and you'll be able to go."

She pounded on the door one more time and then there was quiet.

My sisters and I knew then that we weren't going to go out after all. I put my knee down, pushed the front door all the way open with my hand. Holding the keys, I let my sisters in and then closed the door. I locked both locks. I put the keys on the kitchen table. My sisters followed me. I was annoyed that they were right on my heels. The three of us filed back into our bedroom, past the bathroom door, still closed. I didn't want to hear my father crying. Our bedroom was right before my parents' room, and that door was now closed, too. I knew my mother was in there. I turned on the radio. I told my sisters to be quiet. We didn't close our bedroom door because we knew that once she came out, our mother would yell at us to open it.

I kept thinking about what my mother had just said to my father.

How could she say that? I kept asking myself. Would she really do that to him? I tried hard not to think about what she said. I kept wishing it was Monday and I could go to school. I wished I could be in school every day.

School is what saved me during those years. It was the one place I could go where I didn't have to hear the two of them fighting. I couldn't wait to get up each morning and go to class and forget about my life at home. But it wasn't always easy to leave the house—and get to school—on time.

# CHAPTER 9

I WAS LATE FOR school a lot during fifth grade, the last year of my father's life. When he wasn't in the hospital, he was home. And when he was home, I was his "cigarette girl."

"Get me some cigarettes, cigarette girl," he would sing.

"I'll be late for school," I would say.

"But I really need them," he would whine.

Every morning he was home, I would wake up, get dressed quickly, and try to leave the house before he was up. But he was always up. Almost every morning he would stop me on the way out and tell me that before I went to school, he needed me to go to the drugstore at the end of the block and pick up his cigarettes. Every day I would wish my mother would tell him to leave me alone, that I couldn't be late for school again. But she didn't.

"Just get him his cigarettes," she would tell me. "Just do what your father says."

I would beg him not to make me go to the store. "I can't be late again," I would tell him. "I'll get in trouble with my teacher."

But he would give me one of those smiles—people who remember him tell me I have his smile—and tell me to hurry up and go.

I would rush to the store with my books and look for the man behind the counter in the white coat who was never surprised to see me.

"A pack of Parliaments, please," I would say. The man would hand me a white paper bag folded over twice. I never opened the bag. I would run back to the house where my father would be sitting in the kitchen waiting for me. Smoking and waiting. He would grab the bag, give me a kiss on the back of my hand, and tell me that if I hurried, I wouldn't be late. I would run the five blocks to school and pray that my teacher wouldn't ask me why I was late again.

One afternoon when I came home from school, I saw him sitting in the kitchen, smoking and looking like he hadn't moved all day. He didn't see me come in. I watched as he pulled a cigarette out of his mouth and put it in the ashtray that was always full. He reached into the white bag and took out a tiny little bottle filled with clear liquid. I was surprised that it wasn't the pack of cigarettes. He unscrewed the top carefully. I was going to ask him what he was doing when I saw him take a needle, put it in the bottle, and then stick the needle into his thigh. He closed his eyes as he pulled the needle slowly out of his skin. After a few minutes, he took the cap, turned it, and then put the bottle back into the white bag. He folded the top of the bag twice and put it back on the counter. He was concentrating so hard I know he didn't see me there. I turned around and walked quietly into my mother's room. She was making the bed.

"Why is Daddy getting a shot?" I asked.

She hesitated.

"Is he sick again?" I pushed.

She looked at me and then turned away. She patted the sheet.

"It's medicine," she said. "Medicine that will help him feel better."

"What's it called?" I asked again.

She took the pillows from the floor and put them next to each other, side by side. I remember thinking I couldn't remember the last time my mother actually made her bed. Usually the blanket and pillows stayed exactly as they were from the night before.

No answer.

"Will it make him better?" I asked.

She folded the blanket at the foot of the bed.

"Yes," she said. "Yes, it will."

I didn't complain the next time he told me to go to the drugstore.

〜:〜

I WAS USED to my father being sick. It seemed he was always going in and out of the hospital. Sometimes I didn't see him for weeks. Every once in a while, one of his brothers would pick me up from our apartment and take me to the hospital to visit him. My mother never came with us. I assumed it was because she had to stay home to take care of my sisters.

My father and mother fought about his doctor all the time. My father told my mother he thought he was a god. My mother hated him. "He's using you," I would hear her tell him, usually before he would go into the hospital again. "Why is he operating on you again?" she would add. And then she would answer herself: "He doesn't know what he's doing. Why are you letting him use you?"

"He's like a father to me," he would respond. "I trust him. He's going to make me better," he would tell her.

There were always people in his hospital room laughing and joking with him. As soon as he saw me enter, he would tell everyone I was his smartest daughter and tell me to count to ten in Yiddish.

"Eyns, tsvey, dray, fier, finef, zeks, zibn, achet, nayn, tsen."

"This is my firstborn," he would brag to everyone. She's just like her father, he would tell them. Maybe even smarter than I am. Then he would laugh.

He never looked sick, and he never wore the funny green gown the man in the bed next to him wore. His gold chain necklace was always hanging out of his shirt. At the end of the chain was a flat gold circle engraved with the Hebrew letter chai, or "life." Its shiny face moved toward me when he leaned forward to kiss me hello. It was the necklace my father wore every day until he died.

A woman with big blond hair was always in the room whenever I came to visit. I didn't know her name, and I didn't ask. She was the one who laughed the hardest at his jokes, and I always wanted to tell her he wasn't *that* funny.

Shut up, I would think. I knew my father would slap me if I said that out loud, so I never did.

I was glad that she never tried to talk to me. Whenever she laughed, I could see a smear of bright pink lipstick on her top teeth. I always wanted to tell her to wipe it off with a tissue, but of course I never did. She always seemed to jump away from his bed when I came in. I would watch my father watch her. Sometimes he would stroke his necklace and hold it against his chest, near his heart. I tried not to think about that. I never told my mother about her. I didn't think she would want to know.

# CHAPTER 10

THE DAY MY FATHER died, I was with his favorite brother and his two children—the cousins closest to my age—in the Bronx. My uncle had picked me up from our apartment that Friday after school, and he told my mother he would bring me back late on Sunday night.

Early Sunday morning, a phone call stopped our playing. I could hear my uncle and aunt whispering, but I didn't know they were whispering about me. I was to be driven home immediately, my uncle told me, but I wasn't told why.

I didn't want to go home. I never wanted to go home.

I was used to sleeping at other people's houses. And I

never said no to an invitation to sleep over at this uncle's apartment.

In the car on the way home, my uncle asked me if I loved my father.

"Of course," I said. What a stupid question, I thought.

I watched him as he drove and all of a sudden I realized he looked so much like my father. The same nose, the same chin. People would always tell me I have my father's chin. He even sounded like him when he talked. How did I not notice this before?

There was silence the rest of the trip home.

As soon as the elevator door opened on our floor, my sisters ran out and told me that Daddy was dead.

"Daddy's dead, Daddy's dead," my youngest sister sang. She started to giggle.

"He's dead, he's dead," my middle sister echoed.

I looked at my middle sister. She pushed my younger sister away and shook her head up and down. "He's dead," she said.

Did they understand what "dead" meant? I wondered.

I looked at my uncle. He opened the door to my apartment. He didn't ring the bell.

I followed him in.

My sisters followed me.

There were so many people in our house. I saw my mother talking to people I'd never seen before—some standing, some sitting—all of them crowded around the table where we had dinner every night. My father's best friend, a big fat man who walked with a limp, was sitting in my father's chair.

Get out of that chair, I thought as soon as I came in. That's *his* chair, not yours. As soon as my mother saw me, she called my name. I walked straight into my parents' bedroom, sat on the bed, and started to cry. My sisters weren't used to me crying. You could see they weren't having as much fun watching me in tears as they had a moment ago when they were dancing in the hallway telling anyone who would listen that their father had died.

My mother came in toward me. I started to sob and she patted my back. I wanted her to leave me alone but she kept patting me. I was embarrassed that I was crying. I didn't want anyone to know that I was upset.

# CHAPTER 11

MY MOTHER WOULDN'T let my father's girlfriend come to his funeral.

I didn't know it at the time. All I knew was that my father was dead and my mother was making me go with her to his funeral. Nothing else mattered.

"I don't want to go," I told her.

"You're eleven and you're old enough now," she told me, before we went to sleep. That night, my sisters slept at a neighbor's house down the hall. They weren't going to come to the funeral. They were too young, my mother told me. They won't understand, she explained. My middle sister was almost nine; my youngest sister was almost eight.

I told her I was afraid to sleep by myself, so she let me sleep with her in their bed, on his side.

We woke early that next morning. I watched my mother get dressed in her bedroom.

"You won't ever marry again, will you?" I asked. Not caring that I would be sentencing her to a life without parole, a life that would have nothing but cigarettes and loneliness. And at eleven years old not really understanding or caring about the request and its enormity.

"No, I won't," she said. "I will never marry again."

And she never did.

I don't remember what I was wearing that day. But I do remember that everyone was looking at me, and even though I was eleven and this was my first funeral, I knew that there was something wrong. I was afraid to ask my mother what, though.

I do remember what my mother was wearing. Her beautiful blue eyes were gray that day, dingy and empty gray. And the dark blue dress she was wearing—a shapeless, stretchy, shiny sheath with white stitching on the collar—was one I decided I hated.

I kept looking at the ugly cut the rabbi made on her collar with his scissors or knife—I don't remember which—to remind us of the dead, he said. I was glad he cut her dress. I didn't want to see it on her again, and it stayed in her closet after that day until she died.

She didn't talk to anyone at my father's funeral. And no one talked to her. Or me. I looked for the woman with the big blond hair, the one I used to see in my father's hospital room, but she wasn't there.

I watched my father's brothers watch me. I heard one of them tell my aunt that "she" wanted to come, but that my mother said "she" couldn't.

All of a sudden, I knew who "she" was. I knew they were talking about the blond woman. The woman with the bright pink lipstick on her teeth who laughed too much and was always in my father's hospital room.

My father's girlfriend.

Over her dead body, he said my mother said.

What would I do if my mother were a dead body? I thought. Then I would have no one. Maybe I could live with my uncle, the uncle who looked just like my father. Maybe my sisters could live at the neighbor's house down the hall.

I sat on one of those hard, long wooden benches—the same kind of bench I used to sit in during services in the synagogue—as I was thinking about this. My mother was sitting next to me. I tried to sit still, but the bench was so uncomfortable. I kept twisting my new necklace around my finger.

It was my father's gold "*chai*" necklace. The one he always wore.

When I finished getting dressed that morning, my mother handed it to me and told me to put it on. Told me that my father would have wanted me to have it. I was surprised and thrilled. I knew he loved that necklace and now I felt a little better about going with her. I didn't feel guilty about being happy on such a sad day.

I was surprised my mother didn't tell me to stop fidgeting. She hadn't said a word to me since we arrived.

Soon the rabbi stopped talking and everyone got up and

started putting on their coats. I hadn't taken mine off. Someone announced something about going to the cemetery in Jersey. My mother told me to wait a moment and that she would be right back. She pointed to where I should stand. It was the first time she had spoken to me all morning.

I stood in the corner, and one of my uncles—my father's second oldest brother, I think, the one I saw watching me play with my necklace all through the service—put his hand on my arm and said, "Your daddy loved that necklace."

I looked at him, surprised that someone was finally speaking to me.

"Someone who loved him very much gave it to him."

He paused.

I waited.

"Who?" I asked. And then I realized I knew, and I decided I didn't want to hear.

All of a sudden, my mother appeared. He walked away.

My mother grabbed my hand and pulled me into the hearse. We didn't speak the entire way to the cemetery.

When we got there, I watched a group of men standing around a large, rectangular hole. It was very deep. I could smell the earth. It was pouring rain and I was freezing. I wished I had worn my favorite light blue scarf that day. I was glad someone was holding an umbrella over my head.

I watched while my mother was given a shovel and she bent down, put the shovel in the soil, and then tossed some dirt in the giant hole. She did this once, twice, three times, and then she stepped back and gave the shovel to one of my father's brothers. Each of my father's brothers did the same.

After everyone finished putting dirt in the hole, the rabbi said some words and then the men who had been standing around lowered a long brown box into the hole. I knew my father was in that box.

My mother told me to get into the car that had taken us there. We didn't speak. The car dropped us off in front of our building. We walked into the lobby, my mother pressed the elevator button, and the two of us got in. She opened the door and told me to go into my room and get ready. People were going to be over soon, she said. Don't mess up the bathroom, she told me. I don't want people to think we have a messy house.

I noticed that the mirror in our front hallway had been covered with a white sheet. It hadn't been that way when we left.

I passed by the bathroom and saw that the mirror there was also covered with a white sheet.

I had learned about this in Hebrew school. Something about when a person died, you weren't supposed to look in the mirror. I couldn't remember why, though. And I wondered who had covered up all of the mirrors.

I went into my room, took off my coat, and hung it in my closet. I walked over to my chest with the mirror and saw that it hadn't been covered. I looked at myself.

I opened my top drawer.

I took off my new necklace, put it inside, and closed the drawer. I never wore it again.

# CHAPTER 12

When all of the people finally left the house that day, I
wanted to ask my mother what my father died of. I knew he
had been sick for a long time, but no one had ever told me he
was going to die. I just accepted that he was always going to
go into a hospital and then come back. He always came back.
I knew there was something wrong with how he went to the
bathroom, but I never imagined it would kill him.

But I was afraid to ask. I don't know if I was afraid she
wouldn't tell me—or that she would. I decided I really didn't
need to know.

That night I slept in my own bed, and my sisters slept in
theirs after returning from a neighbor's apartment.

"What happened to our daddy?" my youngest sister asked me. "Will he come back soon?"

My middle sister said she didn't think it was fair that I was able to go to the funeral and that she had to stay home.

"Why did you get to go and not me?" she said. "Why do you always get to do things?"

"Why is he dead?" my younger sister asked. "Will Mommy die, too?"

"I don't know," I told them both. "We don't have a father, but we still have our mother."

I didn't have any friends who didn't have a father.

The next day back at school, a girl in my fifth-grade class called me a "fatherless thing" when I wouldn't let her borrow my notebook. During assembly, I had to make myself think of funny things during the singing of "My Country, 'Tis of Thee" so that I wouldn't cry when we got to "land where my fathers died." I don't know why I would cry during that song. I couldn't help it. I hated telling people I didn't have a father. "What does your father do?" "Do you look like your mother or your father?" Did your father say it was okay?" Somehow, no matter where I was, someone would ask me something that would make me have to admit that he was dead. "I'm so sorry," people would say, when I had to tell them the truth. "What did he die of?" they would always ask. I felt stupid not being able to tell.

Everyone was always so shocked I didn't have a father, and they all wanted to know how old was he when he died and how old was I and how old was my mother and how old were my sisters. When I would tell them that I was eleven and she was thirty-three and he was thirty-four and that my sisters were nine and eight, they were horrified. I didn't want anyone to be horrified. So I preferred not talking about him.

But I always thought about him.

What would he have looked like? Would I have been different? Why didn't he love my mother? Would he like the man I married? Would I live to be older than thirty-four? I decided that my goal in life was to live to be thirty-four.

THE DAYS FOLLOWING his funeral, I wondered what our life would be like without my father. I wondered if my mother and I would become closer—maybe even become best friends. I hoped that would be the case. The good news, I told myself, was that there wouldn't be any more fighting.

Each of those nights my sisters and I would pick through the food gift baskets that were delivered each day to our apartment—I couldn't believe how many baskets there were—and try some of the exotic fruits and chocolates and candies that were packed tightly under the colored cellophane. I was glad my mother didn't yell at us for going through them. Every night we ate food that people sent to us, and the four of us would sit down to dinner together as a family. I took my father's chair at the table. I know my mother noticed, but she didn't say anything.

A week after he died, my mother and I were sitting at the table together. We had just finished dinner and my sisters went into our bedroom to play with their dolls. My mother was making a list of who had sent what and whom she had to send thank-you cards to. She looked around and said she wished we could move to a better place, but that oh, well, it would have to do for right now. I couldn't tell if she was talking to me or to herself. As soon as she looked up, I told her that she was right, that it would be good to move out of this "shit hole"—remembering that was the way she used to describe our apartment to my father.

She looked at me, got up out of her chair, marched down the hall to the bathroom, and came back with a dripping, thick white bar of Ivory soap.

"Don't you ever curse," she said to me, shaking the bar in front of my lips.

"What did I do wrong?" I asked her, shaking my head. "What did I do?"

"Don't you EVER say that word again," she said, standing right in front of me, grabbing with one hand at my sleeve, not allowing me to get up from my chair.

I pursed my lips together as soon as I saw her moving the soap to my mouth. I couldn't imagine that thick white bar of Ivory soap in my mouth.

"Don't you EVER say that word again," she repeated as she pushed the bar against my lips.

I turned away, keeping my mouth shut.

"Open your mouth," she hissed at me. "Your father would kill you if he ever heard you say that word." She kept pushing and twisting the bar against my lips.

I didn't want to remind her he was dead. And I wasn't going to open my mouth.

I kept shaking my head, no.

I kept my lips closed as tightly as I could but I felt the soap grating against my teeth. It tasted horrible and I tried not to swallow.

Finally, she stopped. As soon as she turned away, I tried to spit out the soap and wipe my teeth on my sleeve. Anything to get that terrible taste out of my mouth.

She left me sitting at the table. I waited until I knew she was in her room and then went into the bathroom and brushed my teeth for a very long time. And then I went to bed.

I didn't talk to her for the next few days, and she didn't talk to me. I don't know if my sisters noticed that we weren't talking to each other and I didn't care. I was afraid she would do something else to me and I didn't want to get her upset.

When she wasn't around, I would go through my father's closet and his drawers and touch his clothes and remember what he looked like when he wore them. They still smelled just like him.

Then I would take my red diary, the one he had given me, out of its hiding place and write to myself about how much I missed him and how much I wished he was still here. And how much I hated her.

One day I came home from school and his clothes were gone. Except his belts. She hung them on the outside of each of the closet doors. Just in case we didn't listen, she told us. She wanted to make sure they were handy if she needed them.

A FEW WEEKS after he died, my mother announced she was going to go to work and that she had gotten a job as a switchboard operator at a place called Melody Bra & Girdle. Her office was not too far from where we lived, at the foot of the Queens side of the Fifty-ninth Street Bridge. Because I was the oldest, I was in charge while she was at work. Today we would be called latchkey kids. Back then we were just the kids whose mother had to work and who couldn't play with friends after school because we had to hurry home.

When school finished at three P.M., my sisters and I walked home quickly—no stopping—because my mother would be waiting for my call exactly at three-fifteen. Not a minute after.

She would answer the phone on the first ring.

"You home?" she would ask.

"Uh-huh."

"Did you lock the door?"

"Uh-huh."

"Don't use the stove."

"Okay."

But one day I couldn't stop thinking about the hamburger patties my mother had made the night before. I kept thinking about the taste of Lipton's onion soup mixed into the ground meat. I had to have one of those patties, and I couldn't wait for her to come home at five-thirty. I opened the freezer door and there they were.

But I wasn't allowed to use the stove. But I had to have one.

I looked around the kitchen and saw the shiny silver toaster sitting on the counter. I smiled. I took out one of the patties, wrapped neatly in waxed paper, and held it over the slot. It would fit, no problem. I unwrapped the patty.

I dropped the frozen meat into the slot and pushed down on the lever. After a few moments, the meat popped up—just like a piece of toast! I pressed the lever down again. My sisters, I could see, were impressed.

The smell of the warm meat mixed with the onion soup was almost intoxicating. I could hear sizzling, just like when my mother cooked them! I'm so smart, I thought—and then I noticed the smoke coming out of the toaster. A flame shot up and my sisters screamed my name at the same time. Something in me knew to pull the plug out of the machine. I grabbed the yellow dish towel by the sink, ran water on top of it, and threw it on top of the toaster.

The three of us were quiet.

I took the wet towel off the top of the toaster, looked inside, and saw the ground beef stuck in the coils.

I moved the toaster back to its corner and told my sisters it was time to do their homework.

When my mother got home, she took off her clothes, put on her housedress, and went into the kitchen to make dinner.

"What happened here?" she asked, noticing the wet towel sitting in the sink.

She saw the toaster plug on the counter and gave me one of those tired *now what?* looks. I didn't say anything. And for the first time ever, neither did my sisters.

"What did you do?" she asked.

"I was dying for a hamburger and I knew I wasn't allowed to use the stove."

She looked at me, then looked at the toaster, and then looked at me again.

"I thought it would work," I said, knowing that this was probably my last day on earth. I could see my sisters thinking the same—and they didn't seem to be upset about it.

I watched her while she looked inside the toaster.

"How did you know to pull out the plug?" she asked.

I closed my eyes and waited for the screaming to begin.

"Smart girl," she said. "You're a smart girl."

WHEN MY MOTHER wasn't at work, she was home. After my father died, she stopped going out. She would go to work, she would go to the supermarket, but other than that, she would rarely leave the house.

Except to go to the beauty parlor.

Every Saturday, she would get dressed in blue polyester slacks and a blue and white button-down polyester top, and walk the seven blocks to the salon where her hair would be washed and then tucked into rows of pink plastic curlers with tops that went *click* when they met the bottom tubes. She would then sit patiently under the dryer waiting for the timer to ring. At the sound of the bell, the beautician would take out the rollers, and her hair would be teased into a tower and then sprayed with Aqua Net—back and forth, back and forth—until her lacquered hair looked like a freshly waxed floor and wouldn't move until the next Saturday's appointment. I couldn't understand how she managed to go a full week without washing her hair while mine would start to itch after two days if I didn't wash it.

"I don't like washing it myself," she would tell me. "The week usually goes by quickly," she would add.

After she had her hair done, she would walk back home, take off her clothes, put on a housedress, and then sit for hours at the kitchen table with her pack of cigarettes and endless cups of coffee. I was relieved that she kept her hair appointments after my father died. Even if she didn't go anywhere, at least she was still caring about something and if it was going to be her hair, well, that was just fine with me.

My mother loved her mahogany hair. Not exactly what Clairol had intended, I'm sure, but mahogany was the color that somehow came out of that Nice 'n Easy box once a month on Sunday nights. Mahogany was the color that replaced the dark, rich brown my father had loved. She would put on her blue housedress with the little pink and yellow flowers and the oversized pockets, take out the clear plastic gloves that came in the box with the color packet, and apply the color with a towel wrapped around her shoulders so the dye wouldn't drip onto her dress. She would cover the smelly mixture plastered on her head with a clear plastic shower cap and then sit at the kitchen table and drink coffee and smoke while she waited the thirty-five minutes or so for the color to take. The smell in the house would linger for days.

"It's much cheaper if I do it myself," she would tell us on those Sunday nights when my sisters and I told her that her hair and the house stank. "Besides, they wouldn't know how to get the color right."

OUR LIFE CHANGED a lot in the months that followed. My mother's parents visited all the time. Whenever the phone rang, it was my grandmother. My mother and her mother were so close. It seemed my mother didn't do anything without asking her mother first.

My mother's mother was so different from my father's mother.

She had dark black hair that looked like she went to the beauty parlor every day, not just on Saturdays like my mother, and she had beautiful jewelry my mother always admired. She would ask my mother what she was doing and then tell her what she thought she should do. She was always telling my mother what to do. And it seemed like my mother always listened. My grandfather used to laugh and say the two of them were just like sisters.

Every Saturday night my mother played poker with her parents and their friends. There were always old people in the house. They were always telling my sisters and me to be quiet.

And everyone smoked.

My father learned to smoke in the army, and my mother told me he taught her as soon as he came home. After he died, I didn't see my mother without a cigarette. Our house was always filled with ashtrays with different lipstick colors on all of the stubby little butts.

My sisters and I stayed in our room on poker nights so that we didn't have to smell the smoke. I think my grandmother was the only one who didn't have a cigarette hanging out of her mouth when I would peek in to see if they were just about ready to go home. My sisters and I couldn't wait to eat the leftover cakes and cookies that were brought by my grandparents and their friends. As soon as everyone left, just past midnight, we would wait for my mother to wash up and go into her room to sleep, and then we would sneak into the kitchen to see what was left to eat.

I never told my sisters that my grandfather left money for me on those nights. He would put whatever change he won in a cup on the top of the refrigerator, and when my sisters went back into our room, I would go back into the kitchen, reach up to where he left the cup, and put the coins in my pocket. I would go into the bathroom, close the door, and count out the change. I hid his winnings in a cigar box he gave me that I kept in the back of my dresser drawer. When the box was filled, I would take my money to the bank and give it to the teller with my passbook. I loved watching the numbers in my bankbook go up and up. I couldn't wait to call him the next morning and thank him.

My grandmother always answered the phone and, as soon as she heard my voice, passed the phone to my grandfather.

"Tell your mother to call me later," she would tell me before my grandfather would get on "Don't forget," she would remind me.

My grandfather would wink at me the next time he came to visit and ask me if I was saving my money. "You're special," he would whisper to me. "You're going to do great things when you grow up."

I COULDN'T WAIT for poker nights.

On those nights, my sisters and I found ways to make the time go by until we could come out and eat. Sometimes we would sing to each other and make up little plays. We loved singing the song "If Momma Got Married" from the movie

*Gypsy.* We loved *Gypsy* and watched it whenever it was on television. I wasn't sure whose mother was better—or worse—Gypsy's or ours. But for some reason, we pretended we were singing about our own mother. My mother had bought the record, and we played it over and over on our little phonograph so I could write down the words to the song.

We would take turns singing. First me:

> *"If Momma was married*
> *We'd live in a house*
> *As private as private can be*
> *Just Momma, three ducks, five canaries*
> *A mouse, two monkeys, one father, six turtles*
> *And me.*
> *If Momma got married."*

Then my middle sister:

> *"If Momma was married*
> *I'd jump in the air*
> *And give all my toe shoes to you.*
> *I'd get all those hair ribbons*
> *Out of my hair*
> *And once and for all*
> *I'd get Momma out too."*

Then the two of us together:

> *"If Momma got married."*

We would tell my youngest sister she could sing something else. Sometimes we would fight about who had the better voice. And who was going to be famous when we grew up.

My sisters and I were almost the same age, and people would always tell us how lucky we were that was the case. There were a little more than two years between me and my middle sister, eleven months between my middle and youngest sisters. The three of us would take turns ganging up on each other—two against one. Sometimes my middle sister and I would be the best of friends and do everything we could to ignore my youngest sister. Sometimes my middle and youngest sister would turn against me. It was rare that the three of us would be friends at the same time.

I didn't feel close to either one of them.

"Two's company, three's a crowd," my mother would always say.

And then, "Be nice to each other. You're all you have."

My sisters were my companions and they were my enemies. Sometimes they told on me and sometimes they didn't. After my father died, I found it easier to spend time with them than with friends who expected answers to questions. I didn't want to get close to anyone. I didn't want anyone to know what I was thinking or what I was feeling. I didn't want anyone to feel sorry for me. And my sisters were always there.

Everyone compared us.

I was the smart one, my middle sister was the pretty one, and my youngest sister was my middle sister's sister. I always felt sorry for my youngest sister. I couldn't imagine being known as anyone else but me.

My sisters and I rarely talked about my father after he died. Sometimes it seemed as though I had had this secret life with him, and now that he was dead, it was like he never existed. I knew they didn't have the same relationship with him and I wondered if they were jealous. Or if they even noticed. They were always in the background as far as he was concerned. At least that's how it looked to me.

People would always remind us how good it was that we had each other.

"You'll never be lonely," they would tell us.

"You'll always have someone to play with," they would say.

"And how wonderful that you're all almost the same age," they would exclaim.

I never understood what they were talking about. I never wanted to have a sister. Or two. I just wanted a pet.

I had always wanted a pet, and while my father was alive, I wasn't allowed to have one. Something about having enough to worry about while keeping track of three kids. My mother would chime in, "I already have enough animals in the house!"

A few weeks after he died, I asked my mother if she would please let me have a pet. I was eleven years old, I told her, and responsible. I really wanted a hamster, I told her. A friend of mine had one and it was easy to take care of. It didn't make any noise and it stayed in its cage. It wasn't expensive to feed, either. I would pay her back, I told her. As soon as I got a job, I would pay her back.

She laughed. "I can't believe you want a rodent," she told me. "It's like a little mouse or rat."

"I really want one," I told her. I swore I would keep our room clean so she would never have to come in and see it.

I was surprised when she agreed.

That Saturday morning, my sisters and I went to the pet store to pick out the hamster I had already decided we would name Vanessa. I had heard that name on a television show and loved it. I didn't care if the hamster was a boy or a girl.

Before we left, my mother took some money out of her purse and said to make sure I gave her back all of the change. And she reminded me she never wanted to see that thing and that my room better stay clean or else.

At the store, I decided it wasn't right to have only one hamster for the three of us. And I didn't want Vanessa to be lonely. So I told the man behind the counter that we wanted two more hamsters—and told my sisters we would name each of them Vanessa, too. This way she'll never know we have more than one, I told them. I made them swear they wouldn't tell her.

"We're going to get in trouble," my youngest sister whined.

"No, we won't," I said. "Not if you don't say anything. Don't you want your own hamster?"

I could hear the radio when we came home. My mother was in the kitchen doing the dishes.

"Don't come near me with that rodent," she yelled as soon as she heard the door open. "Take that thing in your room. And then come back and give me the change."

The next few days my sisters and I would rush home from

school to play with our three new pets. The man from the pet store had told me how to clean the cage and how much to feed them. We loved watching them take turns on the hamster wheel—loved hearing the *squeak, squeak, squeak* of one of the Vanessas going around and around.

That Saturday evening, we were playing in our room when all of a sudden we heard screaming from the kitchen. I could hear my name being yelled by my mother. I rushed into the kitchen and saw all of the adults sitting with their feet up, or standing on chairs.

"A *mayzl, a mayzl*," my grandmother was screaming in Yiddish.

"There's a mouse in the house," my mother kept saying, standing on the chair still wearing her slippers.

I realized what had happened.

"No, no," I tried to tell her. "There's no mouse. It's my hamster. Her name is Vanessa. I guess she escaped."

My middle sister came into the room.

"Vanessa escaped," I told her. "We have to find her."

"Vanessa escaped?" She sounded excited.

Her voice got louder. "Vanessa escaped?"

"Yes, Vanessa escaped," I repeated. I motioned for her to be quiet.

"Which one?" she asked.

I shook my head.

My mother screeched, "WHICH ONE? YOU MEAN YOU HAVE TWO OF THOSE FUCKING RODENTS IN YOUR ROOM?" She shook her lit cigarette at me, the ashes falling all over the front of her housedress.

My grandmother started screaming again.

"Ma," my mother told her mother. "Ma, be quiet. It's not a mouse."

"No," my middle sister said. "We have three. One for each of us. It was her idea." She pointed at me.

"I'm going to kill you," my mother said, waving her finger at me. "Find that thing now and get them all out of my house, NOW."

I crouched down and looked on the floor. I saw the hamster under the couch. I coaxed it out, picked it up, and stroked its soft fur. It was shaking. I was sure it was because of all of the screaming.

My mother started to scream again.

"Get out of here with that thing and get in your room and close the door NOW."

I wanted to tell her that I didn't want Vanessa to be lonely. But I knew she wasn't going to listen to me.

THE NEXT MORNING, I went back to the pet store alone. My mother told my sisters they couldn't come with me.

I told the pet store man that my mother said I couldn't have the hamsters anymore.

He said he couldn't give me back my money.

When I came back to the apartment, my mother looked at me and shook her head. "You're just like your father," she said. "You only do what's good for you. You take after him and his goddamn family."

# CHAPTER 13

WE DIDN'T SEE MY father's family all that much after he died. I knew my mother wasn't close to my father's family, so I wasn't surprised. I used to hear my mother tell her own mother that she wanted no part of his family and that she was happy to have no contact with them. She didn't care if she never saw them again. "They're all lowlifes and liars," she would tell her mother. "Every single one of them."

Sometimes she would tell me she didn't want me turning out like any of them. "You have no idea how bad they are," she would tell me when I would ask her why we didn't see them. I missed my cousins, but I was afraid to tell my mother this.

I also missed going to my father's mother's house on Passover. My father had died a few weeks before Passover.

When my father was alive, his brothers and sister and their families made Passover the one holiday when everyone would get together. My grandmother always worried that there wouldn't be enough chicken soup. My cousins and sisters and I couldn't understand how hard could it be to figure out the right amount of soup for everyone, especially since she knew exactly who was coming. Each time the doorbell would ring and another family member would enter, she would add water to the boiling pot. To make sure there was enough soup for everyone, she would say. My sisters and I would call her soup the "greasy water soup." But we would look forward to it every year.

After his death, there were no more Passover dinners at his mother's house.

Sometime after his funeral, my mother told me we were invited to a cousin's bar mitzvah, on my father's side. One of his brothers had convinced her it would be good for her girls to see the rest of his family. That she couldn't keep us all away from them forever. Her husband, my father, wouldn't have wanted that. I was surprised when she told us we were going. But I was thrilled and couldn't wait to go.

My sisters and I had such a good time there. We ran up and down the halls of the catering hall with my cousins, sneaking into other families' receptions and then into the ladies' room where we would watch all of the women reapply their lipstick, fluff their hair, or adjust their stockings—and then mimic them as soon as they left. My uncle, the one whose apartment I was in the day my father died, tried not to laugh when he told us that we better cut it out and that he wouldn't save us when the cops came in to throw us out in the street.

"It's cold out there," he reminded us. "They'll throw you out without your coats and you'll be sorry."

Of course we didn't believe him and of course we didn't care. We were having so much fun and nothing was going to stop us from having a good time.

Later in the evening, when we were all back at the children's table, I saw that most of the adults were dancing. My mother, however, was sitting by herself at one of the tables, smoking. I wanted to go by and show her the bracelet my cousin let me wear for the evening, but I wanted to dance with my cousins first. I hoped we wouldn't have to go home for a long, long time.

Too soon, my mother came up to me and my sisters with our coats. She told us to put them on and to get ready to go. When my father was alive, he was the one who drove us everywhere. My mother didn't know how to drive and didn't learn until much, much later, when she was fifty years old. She told us that she was sure that someone would give us a lift back to our apartment and that we should be ready.

We stood in our spring coats watching while everyone started to leave. I noticed that my father's brothers weren't looking our way. It reminded me of my father's funeral. The uncle who had been laughing with us earlier was the first to go. He didn't say good-bye. I watched my father's sister leave soon after. I heard her tell someone she had a long ride back to Jersey and that, as it is, she's already going to get home past one A.M. and she's having company the next day and she can't believe she's got to do the driving now as her husband says he's too tired and he didn't want to come to this goddamn bar mitzvah anyway. I wondered why no one was volunteering to drive us home. Earlier in the day, we had convinced my mother to take a taxi to the reception—she hated spending money on taxis. It was cold, we told her, and one of our uncles would drive us back home when it was over, Ma, come on, Ma, let's take a taxi there, we pleaded. I saw my father's mother sitting in a chair by the door and waiting for a ride, too. My father was always the one who drove her home. She would sit in the front with him and my mother while my sisters and I slept in the backseat.

I heard a couple whispering loudly—I didn't know who they were—about how terrible it was that the "old lady" was sitting there by herself and that none of her sons were taking her home. I knew my father would have never let her sit there. Even for a moment.

Finally, one of the brothers went over to her and told her that he'd squeeze her into his car.

Now all of my cousins were gone. No one had said goodbye.

We were still waiting.

And then my mother announced we would take a taxi home and the hell with all of them. I'd never seen her so angry.

It was freezing outside. Our thin coats weren't warm enough. We waited a long time for a taxi to come. My mother was smoking cigarette after cigarette. As soon as she finished one, she would light another. I shoved my hands into my coat pockets, they were so cold. I wondered how my mother could keep her hands out of her pockets—and without gloves—for so long. I noticed that her nose was running and she didn't use a tissue. I wished I had a tissue in my pocket to give her. Finally, a taxi stopped in front of us. She took a long drag on her cigarette and dropped it on the pavement without stamping it with the toe of her shoe as she usually did. She told us to get in the back and gave the driver our address. When it was time to pay the fare, my mother counted out the change one coin at a time. I didn't care that it was taking a long time. It was nice and warm in the back of the car and my hands were finally able to come out of my pockets.

The driver called her a "cheap bitch." She dropped her change purse on the floor, picked it up, and then told us to get out of the taxi. Now.

Inside our apartment building, we took the elevator upstairs, and the four of us were silent the four flights up. When we got to our apartment door, my mother looked in her bag for her keys. She couldn't find them. We watched while she opened every zipper and pocket looking for her keys. Shaking, she turned her bag upside down. Everything fell out—her lipsticks, her crumpled tissues stained with different shades of red lipstick, her brush, her comb, her red plastic address book, two unopened packs of cigarettes, a couple of loose cigarettes, her folded plastic bonnet she kept in her bag just in case of rain, the white-net bag of pastel-colored Jordan almonds that was left at everyone's plate at the bar mitzvah, pens and pencils, her little change purse—coins fell every-where—but no keys.

She started to cry.

"Don't cry," I told her. I had never seen my mother cry before.

She kicked the door.

My sisters and I were quiet. We didn't know what to do.

"Where did I put my keys?" she kept asking herself. "Where did I put my keys?"

"Maybe they fell out when you paid the taxi," I told her. I was trying to be helpful.

She told me to shut up and then instructed the three of us to sit on the floor by our door.

"Don't talk," she said. "Don't say a word."

It was hot in the hallway. I took off my coat. I didn't want to ruin my dress, so I sat on top of my coat. I wished we hadn't gone to the bar mitzvah. My sisters were starting to fall asleep. They were both still in their coats, leaning against each other.

We heard the elevator door opening. It was our neighbors from across the hall. She was wearing a beautiful red dress and high, high heels. He was dressed in a tuxedo. The hall was now filled with her perfume.

"What's this?" she asked my mother. Her voice sounded like she was singing. "Is everything all right?"

My mother nodded. You could see she was embarrassed.

My sisters opened their eyes.

"Can you believe it?" my mother said. "We just came home a few minutes ago from a reception and I can't seem to find my keys." She was crouching on the floor, picking up all of the things that had fallen out of her bag and shoving them back in while she was talking to her.

My sisters and I looked at each other. It was three o'clock in the morning according to my pink Cinderella watch. We had been sitting in the hallway for almost three hours.

We were invited in to their apartment to use their phone to call the locksmith. I looked at the couch in their living room. It was velvet like ours, but it wasn't covered with plastic as was ours. I was so tired I could barely stand. I wanted to go sit on their couch, but I knew to just stand by their door.

My mother told the locksmith to wait a minute when he finally got the locks open. She didn't have any cash, she told him, but she would write him a check. He told her she should have told him she didn't have any cash. He didn't want a check. He wasn't going to be able to get his money now until the check cleared and that could take days. She said she was sorry but that's all she had. I saw her hands were shaking. Finally, he grabbed the check from her and left. She locked the door. Both locks.

My sisters and I went straight into our room to sleep. I knew my mother wouldn't yell at us for not washing up and brushing our teeth. Not tonight.

That night, I decided I would never depend on anyone to drive me home. I didn't want to be like my mother.

# CHAPTER 14

WE DIDN'T TALK ABOUT the bar mitzvah or the lock ever again. In fact, my mother and I didn't talk about a lot of things. I wanted to have a good relationship with her. I wanted to have the same kind of relationship with my mother that many of my friends had with theirs—going shopping together and telling each other secrets. But I didn't. I couldn't. Whenever I took a chance and told her a little something about me—about someone who said something mean to me or about a stupid thing I did that I wished I hadn't—she inevitably turned my words against me, and I would end up writing in my diary that I hated her and would never confide in her again. But I couldn't keep that promise for long. I didn't have anyone else.

MY MOTHER DIDN'T sleep a lot in the years after my father died. She would stay up for hours watching television and smoking. I found I had a hard time sleeping as well, and I would lie in bed wondering what she was thinking about during those hours. And wondering what would happen to the four of us. Sometimes I would go into the bathroom with a book, turn on the light, and read until I was too tired to read anymore. Then I would go back into my bed and wait for the morning to come.

Sometimes, if I didn't have a book I felt like reading, I would tiptoe as quietly as I could to get as close as possible to the living room, where my mother couldn't see me, sit on the floor, and strain to hear what was on the television set that was always on. At some point during the night, my mother would get up—to get another cigarette or go to the bathroom—and she would notice me sitting there.

"Go to sleep," she would whisper. "Get back into your bed." But I knew that if I shook my head and told her I couldn't sleep, she would invite me to sit with her on the couch in the living room.

"For just a few minutes," she would tell me. "You can stay until the commercial."

But during the commercial, I would tell her about some problem I was having at school. About someone who said something mean to me. About a boy I had a crush on. Whatever it was, late at night when it was just the two of us, she would listen to me as though I were an adult and make me feel that no matter what, everything would turn out fine.

It was an unwritten rule that we would both stop talking as soon as whatever show we were watching came back on. I think we both needed that break. Sometimes late at night, while we were watching television and talking, she would iron. Standing at the ironing board, she would invite me to get up from the couch and watch how she did each piece of clothing—how she angled the iron to make sure that a shirt collar would end up looking as crisp as if it had come from the local Chinese laundry or how to use just enough starch so that the same white shirt would keep its shape for days after it was worn. I loved hearing the hiss of steam when the starch hit the hot iron. Ironing looked like so much fun. I would ask her to show me how to iron something that was complicated and she would cover my hand with hers while we would go back and forth over whatever we were ironing together. When I told her I wanted to take over the ironing, do it all myself, and have her pay me, I was surprised that she agreed.

"You're not going to burn anything, are you?" she asked.

I never did.

In the beginning, she would give me only one or two things to iron, like a light blue handkerchief with my father's initials that I never understood how it ended up in the laundry week after week. Or one of my sister's white undershirts. We both knew she was testing me. Then I graduated to her housedresses. After that, once a week, she would leave a pillowcase with all of the clothing that needed to be ironed in a corner of the living room, and we both knew I was expected to do all of it.

Once a week I would give her a handwritten bill. She would glance at it and then go to her pocketbook and count out what she owed me.

I loved ironing. As soon as I finished one piece, I would hand it to her and she would put it in a neat pile on the couch next to her. I would iron item after item late into the night. There was something so peaceful about those nights. I felt so grown-up and so important. I would think about how lucky I was to have that time with her. Just the two of us.

But then the next day, or a few days later, we would fight about something—anything—and she would use whatever I told her late at night to make her point about what a terrible person I was.

"No wonder your friend doesn't like you," she would hiss. "No wonder that boy doesn't want to talk to you." She would hurl the secrets I shared with her right back at me, and I would get angry at myself for forgetting she always did this to me. When I would confront her, she would promise she would never do that again, and I wanted so much to believe her. Daughters were supposed to confide in their mothers, I would tell myself. I would remember the fights she used to have with my father. Now that he wasn't around, I guess she needed someone to fight with. And that was going to be me. She knew I loved him more and this was going to be her way of getting me back. I wasn't going to let her treat me like my father. I would never tell her that I was upset, though. Instead I turned to my red diary and told it what I would never admit to her.

Whenever she got angry at me—if I didn't clean my room, if I was on the phone too long, if I didn't put the milk back in the refrigerator—she threatened to go after me with one of my father's belts. Then she would tell me to stand in the corner until I was ready to apologize. I never apologized. I always had a book with me, and as long as I had my book, I could stand in the corner for hours. Reading. And I didn't feel a thing when she hit me.

Reading was my escape into another place. As soon as I finished one book, I started another. I would eat dinner with a book on my lap, putting my fork down to turn the page. I spent hours in the school library and the public library a few blocks from our apartment building. I read everything the librarians recommended, and I would read books I loved over and over so I wouldn't forget them. I would also read anything my mother was reading—magazines like *Reader's Digest,* or books she kept hidden in her pocketbook, like *Peyton Place* or *Valley of the Dolls.* At night, I would take those books out of her bag and read them either in the bathroom or under the covers with the flashlight I took from the junk drawer in the kitchen and kept hidden under my bed. In the morning, I would sneak them back in her bag so she wouldn't know that I had taken them. I was always dying to ask her to explain some of the things in the books that I didn't understand. But I knew she wouldn't tell me. Books were where I learned about places I wanted to go and people I wanted to meet. And what I wanted that I didn't have.

My mother was always telling me to stop reading, to live in the real world. To go play with my sisters. Or watch TV. Put that book down already, she would tell me. All that reading would ruin my eyes, she would warn.

"And you won't look good in glasses," she would add.

# CHAPTER 15

As I MOVED INTO my teenage years, my mother and I fought all the time.

"You're just like your father," she would always say during those fights. That was her big insult to me. "You think everything should go *your* way," she would add, as if I had some nerve assuming so.

Sometimes I would start the fights.

"You're right," I would tell her. "Why shouldn't they go *my* way? Why should I be like you? Why are you so willing to just settle?"

What was wrong with wanting more?

I wanted her to understand. But she couldn't. I didn't want to have her life, and she knew it, and it bothered her. In some ways I also reminded her of my father, I think, and I knew she hated me for that. He, too, it seemed, wanted to escape his life—and hers.

Her blue eyes flashed navy during our fights. And when she got that angry, I knew if I didn't move out of her way, she would hit me with whatever she could find. Sometimes I wasn't fast enough.

One Friday afternoon, I was getting ready to go to a birthday party that was starting at four o'clock. I had just turned thirteen that past Wednesday, and the party was in the building across the street. My friend was also celebrating her thirteenth birthday. The weekend before, a giant snowstorm had overtaken the city, and it seemed as if the entire city had shut down, especially Queens, where the streets sat unplowed for days. By that Friday, the day of the party, I was so happy to leave the apartment and have something fun to do. My sisters were going to stay over at a neighbor's house, and my mother told me she was happy to have a few hours of peace.

Because of the snow, my mother wasn't able to go out and get a birthday cake for me, since the local bakeries were still closed. So that Wednesday, she and my sisters sang "Happy Birthday" to me over a defrosted Sara Lee chocolate swirl cake with two candles, all that she could find in the drawer. I didn't care. I knew I had this party coming and that everyone there would sing for me, too. As I got ready, I couldn't decide what to wear and kept trying on outfit after outfit, going back and forth into the bathroom to see how I looked in the mirror.

I left all of my rejections piled in a corner on the bathroom floor. When I finally did decide, I rushed out of the apartment so I wouldn't be late. I called out to my mother to tell her I was leaving and that I would clean up everything as soon as I got home.

But I forgot. I came home from the party at seven o'clock with an extra piece of cake my friend's mother gave me in celebration of *my* birthday. As I opened the refrigerator door to put it inside, I found my mother behind me. She grabbed my hair and told me she had been waiting for me to come back all afternoon and pick up my clothes in the bathroom and how dare I leave them for her.

"Do you think I'm your maid?" she screamed at me while still pulling my hair. "Do you think I have nothing else to do but to clean up after you while you go to a party?"

She let go. My head hurt. A lot.

I told her I would do it in a minute.

She grabbed my hair again and told me to get in there now. I tried to push her away from me, but she was stronger. I was furious. When she finally let go, I bent over and reached into a drawer, wanting to find something that would make her get away from me. I pulled out a knife.

"I'll kill you," I told her, shaking, pointing the knife at her. "I'll kill you if you ever touch me again." For a moment, the two of us stared at each other—and then she turned her eyes away from mine. She got ready to say something, stopped, and then walked out of the kitchen, toward her room. The house was quiet. I wondered if I really could have hurt her with the knife. And then I wondered what would happen to me—and to us—if I did. I put the knife back in the drawer and closed it.

I went to the refrigerator, opened it, and poured a glass of orange juice. It tasted bad, and I threw it in the sink. I took the piece of birthday cake that was covered in plastic wrap and threw it in the garbage. I knew I wasn't going to be in the mood to eat it now. I went into the bathroom to brush my teeth. I looked in the mirror and didn't recognize the person who looked back at me. I brushed my teeth, patted my face with cold water, and then sat down on the closed toilet seat. I put my head down on the edge of the sink, my arms covering my head. I don't remember how long I sat there.

When I got up, I picked up all of my clothes, walked into my room, dropped them on the floor, and got into my bed. I was glad my sisters weren't home. I opened the book I had been reading to the page that was turned down at the top corner. I lifted the flap, tried to read a few sentences, and then turned it back down. I let the book drop on the floor, closed my eyes, and fell asleep.

I was asleep for only an hour when my mother came into my room and ordered me to leave the apartment. She said I couldn't use the phone to call anyone and told me that if I wasn't out of the house in fifteen minutes she would call the police and have them take me away. She said she was going to go back into her room, and that if I was still there in fifteen minutes—and she showed me her watch, pointing at the time when the fifteen minutes would be up—she would call them.

I didn't believe she would really do this, but I didn't want to take any chances. I didn't know where to go. It was eight-thirty at night. I put some clothes in a shopping bag and then went into her wallet and took out all of the singles. I didn't touch any of the tens or fives. I was glad she left her pocket-book on the kitchen chair. I was going to leave a note for my sisters, but I changed my mind. I didn't know what to write. I left the apartment, closed the door, and walked a few feet away from the front door. I wondered where I was going to go. And then I walked to the far end of the hallway and knocked on my neighbor's door, the old woman whose daughter had given my mother her prized Lladró statue and crystal bowl years ago.

When the woman looked out the peephole and opened the door, I asked if I could please visit with her for a day or two. "And please, please, please don't tell my mother I'm here," I begged. I could tell she wasn't sure about letting me stay, but I promised her my mother wouldn't be upset. I told her my mother wasn't feeling well and that I didn't want to bother her. I wasn't surprised when she agreed, since I knew she was lonely and I would be good company. That night as I went to sleep on her couch, I took pleasure in knowing that my mother had no idea where I was and that I was actually right down the hall. The next morning, as soon as I got up, I called home, and when my mother answered the phone, I hung up. I tried again, and when my youngest sister answered, I hung up. I knew she would tell my mother I had called. I waited to hear my middle sister's voice, and when she finally answered I asked—as nonchalantly as possible—if my mother was asking about me.

"Nope," she said. "She hasn't said a word about you."

I asked her if my mother told her what had happened.
My sister said she didn't.

"Where *are* you?" she asked. "And what *did* happen?"

I ignored both questions.

"You sure?"

"Uh-huh. It's been quiet here. Really quiet," she said.

On Sunday afternoon, I decided to return to the apartment, telling the old woman that my mother was much better now, thank you, and that it was nice spending time with her. And that she didn't need to say anything to my mother about my being there, as I already told her. She told me to come visit anytime—and she hoped it would be soon. And to please thank my mother for sending me in to take care of her.

I opened the apartment door with my keys. Since it wasn't a workday, I knew my mother would be sitting at the kitchen table. Smoking. I didn't say hello and neither did she. I went straight into my room. Later when we would see each other—in the kitchen or on the way to the bathroom—neither one of us would acknowledge I had left. She never asked me where I went.

Sometimes after a big fight, I would call my grandparents, my mother's parents, when my mother was in the bathroom or in her room, and whisper to them to let me live with them. Please, please, please, I would beg. My grandmother, who usually answered the phone, would tell me to be a good girl and to listen to my mother. I would tell her that I was going to run away and disappear forever. She would tell me I didn't mean that and to go play with my sisters.

And then as soon as Saturday morning arrived, my grandfather would appear at our door and tell my mother that he just happened to be in the neighborhood—they lived about twenty minutes away—and that he and my grandmother wanted me to come visit. He never told my mother that I had called them, and I knew my mother would never say no to him. I wouldn't take any clothes with me, just a nightgown and whatever book I was reading. He would take my hand, and on the way to his car I would tell him that I couldn't live with her anymore. That I hated her. He would shush me and tell me that he knew I didn't mean that. She's had a hard life, your mother, he would tell me. You'll understand when you're a mother.

I'll never be like her, I told him. I'll never treat my child that way, I would say.

When we got to their house, my grandmother would make dinner and the three of us would sit in the little dining area near the kitchen and listen to the radio together. After dinner, we would go into the living room and watch whatever was on television. Sometimes it was *The Jackie Gleason Show,* followed by *The Lawrence Welk Show.* The picture was never clear, and my grandfather would adjust the brass rabbit ears this way and that to try to get better reception. When it was time to go to sleep, my grandmother would get a blanket and a pillow from one of the side tables that sat next to their long, orange couch covered in plastic. Then she would open the magic bed—a Castro convertible that was a couch during the day but became a bed at night—and tell me to have a good night. I loved that bed. It was so big and so comfortable. I loved having the living room to myself. The next morning, after breakfast, my grandfather would tell me it was time to go—I never argued with him—and he would drive me back home.

"She's your mother," he would tell me once we were in the car. "Be *goot* to your mother." He never got rid of his Austrian accent.

I want to live with you, I would tell him. I'll be good, I would beg, emphasizing the "d." I wouldn't be any trouble.

"Be *goot* to your mother," he would repeat. He would park his car and the two of us would walk toward our building. Before we entered, he would give me three dollars and tell me to put it in my piggy bank. "Save your money," he would tell me. "Save as much as you can."

He would then take me upstairs to our apartment, and when my mother opened the door, he had me stand behind him so she wouldn't see me immediately, even though she knew I was there. He would ask her to make him some coffee in the kitchen so that I could slink into my room by myself. If one or both of my sisters were home, I would tell them that I would be moving out soon. Even though I knew they didn't care.

After my grandfather left, the house would be quiet and my mother wouldn't mention my leaving. We would pretend nothing had happened. But we both knew I wasn't going to be there much longer. And we both wanted that to be the case. But I was only thirteen years old. I couldn't leave just yet.

# CHAPTER 16

When I was in ninth grade, I decided to take an admission test for one of the city's top public high schools. The school was in Manhattan, not too far from where my mother and father grew up.

I had never heard of the school, but when I found out that most of my thirteen- and fourteen-year-old friends were planning to take the day off to ride the subway from Queens to Manhattan to take the test, I decided I would go, too.

My friends and I were part of a special group of kids whose academic performance allowed us to skip the eighth grade—going straight from seventh grade to ninth. When my seventh-grade teacher told my mother I was going to skip, my mother told my teacher how proud she was of me and thanked her for being such a good teacher. Later she told me she didn't understand how I turned out so smart and that eighth grade was her favorite year.

I didn't care. And I loved the idea of going to high school in Manhattan, not Queens.

I always loved Manhattan. Back when I was eleven, when my mother first started working at Melody Bra & Girdle, she would call me from the switchboard every few weeks and tell me to take my sisters to meet her in front of her office after work. At five o'clock. On the dot. Sometimes she put me on hold while she took another call and when she got back to me forgot I was there and came back on singing "Melody Bra & Girdle, and how may I direct your call?" to me. "Melody Bra & Girdle," I would mimic back in my best "mother's voice," and as soon as she realized it was me, she would tell me to quit fooling around and to be on time. As soon as I hung up the phone, I would go into the little purse she kept by the phone and take out three tokens to pay for the bus. The three of us would leave our apartment at four-thirty, walk to the bus stop across the street, and as soon as the bus arrived, sit together in the front near the driver, just as she instructed. We were not to talk to anyone, not even the driver. We would get off at the last stop, Queensboro Plaza, walk up the elevated subway stairs, past the token booth, and then down the stairs to the other side, so we wouldn't have to cross the giant street below. We would wait for her in the lobby.

As soon as we saw her, she would tell us to hold hands and

she would lead us back up the stairs to the elevated subway, where we boarded a train and within ten minutes would enter the largest store I had ever seen, called Alexander's. I thought it was amazing that we could go from the subway directly into a store and find ourselves in the basement level, looking through tables of shoes, all pairs attached to each other with plastic ties so it was almost impossible to walk in them when you tried them on to see if they fit. While my mother looked for herself, my sisters and I would go from table to table and pick up shoes we liked—it didn't matter what size. We would put on both shoes and laugh while we tried to walk in them, pigeon-toed, with the plastic attachments. We knew not to go too far away from where my mother was looking, as we didn't want to hear her yell our names in front of everyone if she couldn't see us. After she bought her shoes, she would take us to the main floor and look on tables for dresses or blouses or anything else that looked interesting.

Sometimes when she finished shopping, she would take us to the Chock Full o'Nuts coffee shop a few blocks away, where we would sit at the counter waiting for our sandwiches, going around and around on the stools until my mother told us to stop. I thought the most grown-up thing in the world was to sit at the counter and order a cup of coffee. Black. With a little milk. Just like she always ordered.

One evening, after she finished shopping and we heard the announcement that the store was going to close in a few minutes, a woman started talking to my mother while they were both rummaging through the same table. There was a special on ladies' sweaters. The woman told my mother that we were beautiful children and asked our ages. I was surprised that my mother was talking to her. Usually, when someone talked to her about us—we always got a lot of attention since the three of us were all pretty close in age and height and people sometimes thought we were triplets—my mother would just nod and move on.

I wondered why my mother was willing to talk to this woman. When they finished chatting, my mother made a point of telling us how nice that woman was as we rushed back into the subway looking for the token booth.

When we took the subway with my mother, she never paid our fare. She would push the three of us in front of her and force us to go under the turnstile as she paid for herself. I was always afraid we were going to get arrested, but she would assure me it was fine.

"You're all small," she would tell us. "They won't know how old you are."

But when she went to the booth to buy her token that evening, she realized her wallet was no longer in her bag.

I saw the tears fill up in her eyes.

"She tricked me," she told the woman in the booth. "She took my wallet when she was talking to me." You could see that the woman in the token booth felt sorry for her.

"Go under the turnstile," the woman told her. "Hurry up."

I couldn't believe my mother was going to go under with us.

I couldn't believe she had let that woman take her money.

The four of us were quiet all during the short trip back to Queens.

When we got off the subway, we waited for the bus. As soon as it arrived, my mother waited for all of the other people on line to get on, and then she told us to go to the back.

"Go, go, go." She pushed the three of us into the bus. "Go all the way to the back," she said. "Hurry up."

I turned around as I was walking toward the back and saw her talking to the driver. I didn't want to know what she was saying. I held my breath, waiting to see if he would let her on the bus. He did. She walked to where we were sitting and didn't say anything. She sat down next to me, opened her bag, opened up some of the zippers, closed them, and then sighed. She snapped the bag shut and closed her eyes. I didn't want to see her cry again. I looked out of the window and saw the lights of the Fifty-ninth Street Bridge behind us. I hoped this wouldn't mean we would never come back to Manhattan.

A FEW MONTHS later, when I found out I was accepted into the special high school in Manhattan, I couldn't wait to get home to tell my mother the good news. Not everyone who took the test got in, I told her.

I asked what she thought I should do.

"Why do you want to go there?" she asked me. "The high school here in our neighborhood is fine."

"But it's considered one of the best schools in the city," I told her.

I couldn't understand why she wasn't as excited as I was.

"And it's in Manhattan," I said. "Manhattan, Ma. Manhattan. I'll meet kids from all over the city." I wanted her to be happy for me.

I tried one more thing. "You were born in Manhattan," I told her. "I'm going to school in your old neighborhood."

I thought that might do the trick.

It didn't.

"Do whatever you want," she snapped. "If it doesn't work out, I guess you can always come back here."

I looked at her.

"It's going to work out," I told her. "And I'm not coming back."

WHEN HIGH SCHOOL began that fall, I would leave the house each day at seven A.M., and take the bus and then two subways to the school on Fifteenth Street between First and Second avenues. During the second semester, soon after I turned fifteen, I started my first job. As soon as classes finished for the day, I would take a short subway ride to E. J. Korvette's, a discount department store across the street from Macy's in Herald Square, where I worked as a cashier two days a week. I made two dollars an hour, the same amount I remembered my mother made when she first started working, right after my father died. She told me it was okay to lie about my age and say I was sixteen so I could be a cashier and not have to stock shelves. On the days I wasn't at the store, I worked at a small publishing company, called Johnson Reprint, a few blocks away from my school, filing, answering phones, and doing whatever the ladies in the office told me to do.

I did my homework on the subway on my way back home to Queens. Whenever I had an afternoon off, I would stay in Manhattan as late as possible. Sometimes I would go with my friends to museums. Or to Greenwich Village to go window-shopping. Or to their houses to do homework. I found any excuse to sleep over at my friends' houses. Almost all of them lived in Manhattan or Brooklyn. Only a few lived in Queens. On those nights I would call my mother and tell her I wouldn't be coming home that evening and not to worry, I would see her tomorrow. Or the next day. When I came home, whatever the time, my mother would yell at me for returning late or for not calling her first to see if she needed anything from the store.

"You're just like your father," she would tell me. "You only do what's good for you."

I loved not having to depend on my sisters for companionship and was happy I didn't have to see them too often. Other than our mother, we had little in common. They were mother's girls—I was daddy's girl, I told myself. And none of us had any real desire to get to know each other any better. They were happy to go to the neighborhood high school. They, like my mother, couldn't understand my love affair with Manhattan.

I couldn't understand why my mother, who was born in Manhattan, would have ever moved to Queens.

"Why do we live here?" I would ask her all the time. "When I get older, I'm moving to Manhattan."

"Do what you want," she would respond. "Do whatever's good for you."

And then she would add—sometimes aloud and sometimes under her breath—"Like father, like daughter."

# CHAPTER 17

ALL THROUGH HIGH SCHOOL, my mother and I fought about everything. About nothing. About where I was going and when I was coming back. About whom I was with. About why I was going out and why I was staying home. I counted the days until my eighteenth birthday, when I would legally be able to move out and rent my own apartment. And the more I traveled away from her, from her apartment, from her life and into Manhattan—to go to high school, to go to museums, to explore the streets and neighborhoods—the more confident I became and the more I felt I deserved everything my mother thought was out of her league.

I wanted to leave my mother's gold and green living room with the yellowed plastic covers on the couch and chairs, the plastic that had hardened through the years and would stick to your bare legs in the summer when we didn't have the air conditioner on. The plastic I had tried to tear with my fingernail whenever I thought she wasn't looking. I thought if I made a big enough hole my mother would finally remove it—and I could sit comfortably on the soft, now matted, crushed velvet. The only thing in my mother's living room that wasn't either gold or green was the lamp shades. They were black, black velvet.

"It's more elegant when things match," my mother would tell us when we would try to introduce a new color into the room—anything that wasn't gold or green—waving us off. I would tear out pages from magazines to show her how other people used color and pattern and how pretty those rooms were. I wanted our living room to look like the living rooms in those magazines.

"Why are you reading those things, anyway?" she would sneer. And then she would tell me those people didn't know what they were doing. "You think this looks good?" she would challenge me when I showed her a page I liked. "That's not the way real people live," she would lecture.

"Since when do you know how real people live?" I would laugh.

She wasn't amused.

By then, in 1971, when I was fifteen, we had moved to a co-op housing development across the street from our building in the projects. I had always wished that one day we would move there.

My mother put her name on the list to get into the co-op development a few weeks after my father's death. She always told him she hated living in the projects and he would promise her they would move one day.

A few days after his funeral, I went with her to the co-op's office, where she put her name on a list and wrote a check for a few hundred dollars for the application fee. The woman who took her money told her she had no idea when an apartment would become available, but that when one did, she would have to decide quickly if she wanted it, since there was a long list of people who would take it if she didn't. The woman added that if she didn't take the apartment that was offered, her name would go to the bottom of the list. And good luck to you about getting in then, she told my mother.

My sisters and I would talk about how great it would be when we finally lived in a nice building. I never wanted to tell anyone I lived in a housing project. Finally, I hoped, I would be able to have friends come visit.

When my mother got the call that an apartment was available, she called her mother and asked her how she was going to make the down payment. She didn't know I was listening to her on the phone.

"I think I can handle the rent, but I don't have enough for the down payment," I overheard her tell her mother. "He didn't leave me enough money." And then, "I've got to get out of this shit hole. I can't live here anymore."

Later that day she asked if I wanted to go with her to look at an apartment. She wasn't sure if it would be right for us.

"Are you kidding?" I told her. "Don't you want to live in a better place?" I demanded. "Let's go look at it now."

"It's a lot of money," she told me.

"It's worth it," I told her back. "We need to move out of here."

We walked over to the building, and as soon as she opened the door to what I hoped would be our new apartment, I knew we would have to live there. I couldn't wait for us to move.

The new apartment was clean and quiet. We still had two bedrooms, but now we lived in a building where the elevator worked, we had air conditioners, and the hallways didn't smell like urine. We no longer had to listen to the garbage trucks coming in and out of the garage all night. We could see a small playground from the big window that extended from the dining area to the living room. There was always someone swinging on one of the swings, and my mother would sit for hours drinking her coffee, smoking, and looking out the window.

My middle sister and I shared one bedroom and my mother and youngest sister shared the other. Everyone had a twin bed.

My middle sister and I would tease my youngest sister about sleeping in my mother's room. You're such a mama's girl, we would taunt. And then she would cry. We didn't care. We were happy we weren't the ones who had to share the room with my mother. But we weren't going to tell either one of them that.

ONE DAY, A FEW weeks after we had moved in, my mother and I were sitting at the kitchen table. She was drinking her coffee and I was reading a magazine. I glanced over to the living room and told her I thought it was time for her to make some changes.

"If you don't like living here, leave," she responded, taking a long puff of her cigarette. I waved the smoke away and told her to stop smoking.

"You're never here, anyway," she scolded me. "You come and go as you please and you treat this place like a hotel."

And then, predictably, the line that was intended to hit like a sledgehammer: "You're just like your father."

I smiled. "I'd rather be like him than you," I told her.

My mother looked at me, her eyes narrowing. "Wipe that smile off your face," she screamed at me. "You're a snob. You think you know everything."

She crushed out the cigarette in the ashtray. I knew she would hit me if I didn't get up and out of her way.

"Get out," she screamed. "Get out of my house, now."

I went straight into my room and to the phone on the desk. I called my best friend and prayed that she would answer the phone. I prayed my mother wouldn't follow me.

"Get out," I could hear her screaming from the kitchen table. "Get out, get out, get out, get out." When I finally got my friend on the phone, I tried not to raise my voice and pretended that the noise in the background was coming from someone else's apartment. I could hear my mother coming into my bedroom.

"The neighbors are at it again," I told her. "I'll call you back in a few minutes, okay?" I don't think I fooled her.

"I hate you," I screamed back at my mother when I was

off the phone. "You're a sick person. I'm going to move out as soon as I have enough money."

"Move out now," she responded. "Get out of my house now."

I rushed out of the house as quickly as I could. I grabbed whatever I could find—my schoolbooks, the book I was reading, a clean shirt, a toothbrush, and keys—and went. I always made sure I had money in my purse, money I saved from babysitting, from my grandfather's Saturday night poker winnings, and from my part-time jobs.

After leaving my mother's house, I went to the phone booth on the corner and called my best friend back and hoped she would answer the phone before I ran out of change. Right after she answered, I took the subway to her apartment, where I stayed as long as I could without feeling like an intruder. I tried to be the perfect guest. I didn't want her mother not to want me to come back. I didn't make any noise and smoothed out the towels in the bathroom and left whatever I touched as though it hadn't been touched. I didn't leave crumbs on the table. My friend's mother told my friend she didn't understand why I was always there. But that I was welcome to visit anytime and that my mother was lucky to have such a nice daughter like me.

# CHAPTER 18

I WAS SEVENTEEN WHEN I graduated from high school and decided to attend a local city college. It had never crossed my mind to go away to school. While most of my friends were filling out college applications for some of the best schools in the country during senior year, I knew I would stay in town. I knew that my mother couldn't afford to send me away, and I didn't want to go into debt paying back a student loan. I thought that if I went local, I would be able to work, save money, and move out of my mother's apartment and into my own life.

My mother and I never discussed college. I knew she

wouldn't care whether I went or not. She had gotten a job right after she graduated high school. Whatever I wanted to do with my life was up to me. And I know she assumed I would figure it all out myself.

My four closest friends couldn't understand why I wasn't applying to any "away" schools.

"Don't you want to live in a dorm?" they asked. "Wouldn't it be great to live in a new town or city and really be on your own? Do you really want to stay in the city and take a subway to school?"

And what they didn't say, but I know they thought: "Do you really want to live at home? Do you really want to live with your mother?"

I told them I really wanted to work, save my money, and get my own apartment when I turned eighteen the following year. And that maybe I would change my mind and then apply somewhere else next year. Or maybe the year after that.

And then I changed the subject.

My friends knew I didn't have a close relationship with my mother and that my father had died when I was younger. They also knew that my mother and I fought a lot—but they fought with their mothers, too. Who didn't? I assumed no one imagined my life was any different from theirs. And I didn't want them to think anything else.

All of my close friends were close to their parents, especially their mothers.

One Saturday afternoon I was at a friend's apartment, in her bedroom, and we started talking about our mothers. We had been lying on her bed together reading magazines and talking about boys, and her mother kept coming in—to ask her when she was going to clean her room, to bring us cookies we didn't ask for, to ask her when she was finally going to cut her hair, to remind her to call her grandmother—and she kept telling her mother to leave us alone. Every time her mother left, the two of us would start whispering to each other about how much we hated our mothers and how annoying they were and how we were positive that when we were mothers we would be different and that we would never treat our daughters the same way they treated us. I was so glad finally to be able to tell one of my friends how I really felt about my mother. I told her I would never hit my daughter like my mother hit me. My friend looked so horrified that I immediately laughed and told her I was kidding. That of course my mother never hit me. After that, I never told my friends anything about her.

Sometimes I felt like I had two lives: my high school life and my secret life at home. I felt like a fugitive, afraid I would get caught. I wished my two lives would become one. And I knew the one I wanted.

That fall, I started college and managed to arrange my schedule so that I had classes that began early in the morning and ended on most days by noon. As soon as I finished my last class, I would rush to catch the bus to the subway to the bus that took me to Roosevelt Island, a small block of land between Queens and Manhattan that housed a hospital on either end. I worked as a clerk for one of the doctors at the hospital on the north end of the island. I typed patient reports, answered phones, and wished that I had listened to my mother who told me to learn shorthand, telling me it would come in handy one day. I was lucky that the doctor I worked for spoke very, very slowly so I didn't have to admit I didn't know any official version. I created my own.

On Thursdays, as soon as I finished at the doctor's office, I traveled into Manhattan, where I worked as a salesperson in the junior department at B. Altman's, a department store on Fifth Avenue, until the store closed at eight P.M. I found both jobs posted on the job bulletin board at college. As soon as I saw them, I took the notices off the board so no one else could apply. I made extra money typing papers and was really fast. I put my own ads on the college bulletin board, charging less than anyone else who advertised typing services. I had used some of the money I made to buy an IBM typewriter so I could type papers at home in my spare time.

I loved working. And making money. My goal was to make as much money as possible so I could afford to move out of my mother's house. I decided I was going to find an apartment and move out before I started my sophomore year.

The only one I told my plans to was my grandfather. I was so busy with school and work that I didn't have a chance to see him in person. But I called him whenever I could—just to hear his voice and to hear him tell me how proud he was of me. He would ask me about my different jobs and how much I was making and saving. I never called him when my mother was around and didn't tell her when we spoke. I knew he wouldn't tell her either.

During the Christmas holiday, my mother told me he had been diagnosed with emphysema and she admitted to me she was worried about him. When he entered the hospital, I asked her if she thought he might die, and she said she didn't know. All she would tell me was that he wasn't doing well but that I shouldn't worry about it. He would be fine.

He died in January at the beginning of the second semester of my freshman year, a month before my eighteenth birthday.

I couldn't imagine what it would be like without him. I couldn't believe he wasn't going to be around to act as the shield between my mother and me. He was the one person I trusted to be there for me, no matter what.

After his funeral, my mother and I didn't talk about my grandfather. We couldn't. We were both living with our own grief, and it was unspoken that we didn't want to admit to each other that we had this one thing in common.

We went about our days following his death managing to keep out of each other's way. After my grandfather's death, I thought we had reached a point that we would be able to co-exist. And given my classes and work, I assumed my mother and I would have very little time to see each other. And no time to fight.

It didn't work out that way.

One Sunday morning, a few weeks after I turned eighteen, I was still in bed enjoying the fact that I didn't have to get up to go to work or school. Before I went to sleep the night before, I told my mother how tired I was and how desperate I was for a good night's sleep and how much I wanted to sleep late the next morning. I asked her not to wake me and she said she wouldn't.

That morning, when I finally awoke, I couldn't tell what

time it was as the shades were drawn and I couldn't see the clock from my bed. I didn't know where my sisters were—I assumed they had gone out together earlier. All I knew was that I was alone in my room and the only thing I heard was the sound of my mother's slippers going back and forth from the kitchen to the bathroom to her bedroom. I wished she would just sit in the kitchen and smoke as she usually did.

All of a sudden, she came through the door to my bedroom and went over to the sliding door closet where my sisters and I kept our clothes and where she kept some of hers. I could hear her rummaging inside.

I kept my eyes closed, not wanting her to know I was awake. I tried not to notice she was there and counted to myself the minutes for her to leave my room.

She didn't leave. I could hear her dig deeper and deeper into the closet. I hated thinking that she might be touching my things and wondered what she could possibly be looking for.

Finally, I could no longer pretend I was sleeping, and I told her to be quiet. And that couldn't she tell I was sleeping and couldn't she look for whatever she was looking for later. I reminded her that I had asked her last night to let me sleep as I was so exhausted from school and work and she said she would. Let me finish sleeping, I begged. Get out of my closet, I told her.

And then I whispered to myself: And get the hell out of my room.

Then I opened my eyes.

And I saw her look at me and move toward my bed.

She ripped the covers off my bed and told me to get up. Now. I shook my head and told her to leave my room. Now.

She told me to get up, to get out of bed, and to get the hell out of her house and her life. Now. Her voice got louder and louder and she was screaming and coughing at the same time. She started grabbing things out of the closet and throwing them on the floor. As soon as she touched something, she threw it on the floor. Clothes—some with hangers, some not—were everywhere.

I got out of my bed and tried to pick things up faster than she threw them. She was faster than me.

I screamed at her to stop, but she kept going and going. She reached far into the closet and pulled out the hot pink Samsonite suitcase she had gotten on sale and given to me for my birthday the year before. She pushed it toward me and told me I had ten minutes to pack and to get out, and that she would call the police if I didn't go. Panting, she left my room and told me not to take anything that wasn't mine.

She told me she would wait by the door to the apartment and that she was timing me.

I tried to shove everything I owned into the suitcase. Clothes, shoes, books, stuffed animals. I willed myself not to cry. I was ready to leave when I remembered to take my red diary, the diary that my father had given me years ago and that I had kept hidden all of these years. The diary I turned to whenever my life with my mother was almost unbearable. "Write it down," I would tell myself during those times, remembering that was what my father told me to do whenever I had a fight with someone. He promised me that writing it down would make me feel better—and he was right. The diary was the one place I could tell all my secrets I couldn't tell anyone else.

I went through the drawers and the closet. Under the pillow. Under my bed. Under my middle sister's bed. It wasn't there. I started to panic.

I tore into the bathroom, my mother's bedroom. Went through her drawers and her closet. Still nothing.

"Are you looking for something?" she said. I could hear her voice by the door.

"My diary," I told her. "The red diary Daddy gave me."

The diary that was my comfort, the place I turned to when he wasn't there to help me. The diary I could tell my secrets to and never worry that they would be thrown back at me.

She laughed. "I threw it away," she told me. "By accident."

As soon as she saw me coming, she moved away from the door and watched as I dragged the suitcase with two hands out to the elevator. I couldn't believe how heavy it was. I hoped I hadn't left anything important in the house. As soon as I got to the elevator, she closed the door. My mother didn't say good-bye and neither did I. I was glad my sisters weren't home. I didn't want to have to see their faces. I knew they wouldn't defend me, and even if they did, it wouldn't have mattered. It was time for me to go.

By now I had a car. When my grandfather died, he left me a 1967 dark gray Chevy Malibu that was so big I had to sit on my books to see through the windshield. I used some of the money I had saved to pay for driving lessons. It took me three tries before I got my license because other than my once-a-week lesson, I didn't have anyone to practice with me. I would look out my bedroom window and watch my grandfather's car sit in the parking lot waiting for me.

My grandfather, who always rescued me after the fights with his daughter when he was alive, was helping me again by giving me a way to escape—even in death. His car was my freedom. It got me back and forth from school to my jobs. From my mother's house. And out of her life.

When I got down to my car, I thought about throwing my mother's house keys into the garbage can that was sitting out front. I decided to keep them. The lock for the trunk wasn't working, so I managed to get the suitcase into the backseat and slammed the door shut. I turned on the radio, opened the window, and sped off. I didn't look back.

I drove to a friend's house, where we spent the next few days looking at the ads in the local newspapers listing people who wanted to share their apartments. I found a roommate who didn't smoke and didn't care what I did as long as I didn't eat her food.

I knew that I would never live in my mother's apartment again.

And now I was able to admit what I knew all along: I hated her and didn't care if she hated me back.

All that mattered now was that I was free.

# PART TWO

# CHAPTER 19

My relationship with my mother changed for the better after I moved out. Now that I didn't live with her anymore, I wasn't reminded of all that I didn't like about her. I had to talk to her only if I wanted to—and if I did, I would call her. Sometimes I found I actually looked forward to talking to her on the phone, forgetting about the fight that finally pushed the two of us apart. I had decided I didn't want to remember.

I kept a lot about my personal life from her—and she never asked. I didn't tell her what was happening at school and what classes I was taking. I didn't tell her whom I was dating and if I was happy. I didn't tell her about the different jobs I had through college to support myself. I knew she wouldn't understand why work mattered so much to me.

"It's just a job," she would tell me. "Why do you care so much about a job?"

I didn't want to tell her how much I didn't want to be her. I wasn't going to be a switchboard operator in a bra factory. I wasn't going to depend on my mother to give me money to live. I wasn't going to depend on anyone.

I couldn't wait to finish college and find a permanent, full-time job. A friend had recommended an employment agency, which was impressed by my typing skills. I got a job working as an assistant at a publishing house and was told it could be a stepping-stone to becoming a book editor. It didn't pay a lot of money, but I loved being surrounded by books and the people who cared about them—even though most of my time was spent answering the phone and making copies of manuscripts and getting coffee for my boss, who drank endless cups of it. Every night, I took home a different book and started reading it on the subway ride home. Sometimes I stayed up all night reading. I thought I might like to be a book editor until a friend told me about an ad he had seen in the *New York Times* for an advertising telephone salesperson at the paper.

Growing up, I always thought that people who read the *Times* were smart—not like the people who read the papers my mother read, like the *Long Island Star Journal* and the *Daily News*. Or even the *New York Post*, which had been my father's favorite.

"Why do you want to read that paper?" she would always ask me when she saw me at the kitchen table devouring the

*Times* on Sunday mornings, when I was still living at home. I discovered the paper in high school, when all of my friends and teachers would talk on Monday about what they read over the weekend. Every Saturday night my friends and I would go to the movies—Ingmar Bergman, any French film, any movie that had been written about in the *Times*—and since finding a newsstand in my Queens neighborhood that had it late on Saturday night was hard, I would pick up a copy in Manhattan after the movie and start reading it on the subway ride home. I had to be careful not to miss my stop. On those Sunday mornings, I would read every section from cover to cover. My mother would flip through her *Daily News* and tell me I was wasting my money with that *other* paper.

I LOVED THE idea of working for the *New York Times*—and the job paid twice what I was making in book publishing. I was thrilled when I got the job. Soon after, a colleague told me about an apartment she was leaving on the fifth floor of a walk-up on the Upper East Side. I had been dying to move to Manhattan from Queens for years and finally I found a place I could afford. The kitchen floor sloped, the windows didn't open more than a slit, and the oven didn't work. But I loved it. It was mine, I didn't have to share it with anyone. And it wasn't in Queens.

About two months after I moved in, I decided I wanted my mother to see it. I wanted her to see what I had worked so hard for. Then maybe she would understand.

But would she insist on smoking in the apartment?

All during our life together, her cigarettes were the cause of

so many of our fights. When I was a child, my mother and father would smoke cigarette after cigarette while in the car with
me and my sisters. I used to pray that they would forget to bring
a fresh pack. My sisters and I would sit in the backseat. I would
get carsick every time, even when I sat by the window. As soon
as I felt myself getting ready to throw up, my father would pull
over on the side of the road, and I would get out as soon as the
car stopped. I always carried a roll of Life Savers in my pocket
so that I wouldn't have to smell my breath after I finished. The
only time I didn't get sick was when I sat in the front.

"Why do you have to smoke in the car?" I would ask my
parents before every trip. My father would laugh and tell me
he liked it. "I'll blow the smoke out the window," he would tell
me. "You won't even know I'm smoking," he would add. My
mother would tell me to shut up.

"Can I sit in the front seat?" I would beg my mother. "If I
sit in the front, I won't get sick."

I knew my mother would never switch seats with me.

I dreaded going anywhere in the car with the two of them.

After my father died, my mother promised to quit many
times. For a day or two she would manage to go without a cigarette—at least in front of us. None of us believed she didn't
smoke late into the night, long after she convinced herself
that the three of us were sleeping and not likely to awaken.

Eventually, we would find her sitting at the kitchen table
with her coffee and cigarettes. Smoking one after the next.

As I got older, I would tell her that if she didn't quit, she
would get cancer.

"Then I'll be dead and you'll be happy," she would say with
a shrug.

After I had been living in my Manhattan apartment for over a year, I finally convinced her to come visit me. I had a great new coffeemaker, I told her, and I couldn't wait to serve her a really good cup of coffee. My apartment was filled with red and blue and orange and green on my framed posters and on pillows. I loved seeing so many different colors in the room and was pleased by how they all worked together. I bought a white couch and matching chair. My mother never would have bought anything white for our apartment. She used to tell everyone that her daughters were slobs, that *we* were the reason our house was always a mess. After we all moved out, nothing changed: her apartment was still a mess. I wanted her to see how I kept my own apartment.

I was thrilled when she said she would come.

I gave her the address and told her to take a taxi into the city. It was just a quick trip over the bridge, I said. It wouldn't cost her all that much and she didn't want to have to think about which subway to take, did she?

She agreed to take a taxi and told me she was looking forward to seeing me.

The morning she was supposed to come over, I got up early to buy breakfast for the two of us. I knew she loved fresh orange juice, so I bought two bottles. I got half-and-half for her coffee. I bought a coffee cake at a bakery I knew she would love. I arranged fresh flowers in my living room and bedroom and made sure my bathroom didn't have any hair on the floor. She called me up before she was getting ready to leave and asked me if I needed her to bring anything.

"Just you," I said. "I have everything we need."

And then as we were getting ready to hang up, I heard

these words come out of my mouth: "You know you can't smoke in my apartment, right?"

She didn't answer.

I could feel the mood change, but I pressed on. "You didn't think I would let you smoke here, did you?"

Did I not want her to come?

"You didn't think I would let my apartment smell like yours, did you?" I couldn't stop myself.

Still no answer.

Now I was angry. "Surely you're not saying you can't *not* smoke for an hour or two," I demanded. "That's pathetic."

She broke her silence.

She told me to drop dead and then slammed down the phone. I realized our relationship hadn't really changed at all.

My mother never saw my first Manhattan apartment.

# CHAPTER 20

We didn't talk for months after that, and I can't remember who finally made the call to the other. Or why. When we finally did speak, I didn't talk about my apartment and she didn't ask. And I didn't talk about work.

For some reason, the mere mention of the *New York Times* triggered her anger toward me, long after I moved out of her apartment. Sometimes it seemed as if the *Times* was in some way the cause of our problems.

One Sunday morning, she asked me if I would drive her to visit her mother. As we were pulling out of the parking lot in the back of her building, I told her about an article I had read in the *Times* that morning that I thought was interesting and suggested she read it, too.

"You should really read it," I told her. "It's a great paper. It wouldn't be terrible if you learned something new. And it wouldn't kill you to be interested in something that *I'm* interested in, would it?"

I couldn't stop.

"You know," I said, enunciating every single word, "I work at the damn paper. Would it kill you to actually read it? Would it kill you to make me think you actually have a clue about what I do for a living? Would it?"

She pulled a cigarette out of her bag and put it into her mouth. She knew she wasn't allowed to smoke in my car. She took out a book of matches and tried to light the cigarette. The passenger window was open and the match kept going out. She kept trying over and over to light the match. As I was driving, I looked at her out of the corner of my eye. I wouldn't turn toward her, but I noticed she had polished her nails with a light brown, mocha polish, whatever wasn't chipped off. She was wearing a watch with a thin black band that had a tiny white face with silver numbers. When I stopped at the corner to make a right, I glanced down at that watch. I always knew that she had skinny little wrists, but they caught me off guard when I saw the watch. She had added extra holes in the leather. The watchband extended far out past the little piece that was supposed to hold the band flush against the rest of the leather.

She rolled up her window and used her watch hand to hold the matchbook. With the cigarette hanging out of her mouth, she scraped against the scuffed black edge of the matchbook with a jerky motion. Over and over. Again and again. When she finally got the match to light, she lifted it up to the cigarette and lit it. She inhaled through her nose and then blew the smoke toward me out of the left side of her mouth. I kept my right hand on the steering wheel as I was driving and reached for the window handle with my left. I rolled down my window and didn't say a word. I looked straight ahead as I drove. I stopped at the corner and made a right. And then another. The two of us were silent. She was smoking, and I was watching the road. I still wouldn't turn my head to look at her. I wouldn't allow myself to cough. When we got back to her building, I pulled up and said nothing. She opened her door, slammed it, and walked around the front of the car and toward the entrance to her building.

I don't know why I waited.

She paused, turned around, and walked back to me. I still didn't turn my head. I was looking straight ahead. She leaned into my window so that her head and mine were at the same level.

"You're such a snob," she sneered. "You think you're better than me."

I didn't move. I wouldn't move.

"Who do you think you are?" she said, gritting her teeth, talking through the cigarette. I knew she was trying hard not to cry. I still wouldn't turn my head. The smoke smell was everywhere, even though the window was open. I felt nauseous.

"Who do you think you are?" she repeated. And then she walked away from the car. I waited for her to enter her building. And then I opened my door and threw up. We didn't talk for months after that.

AND THAT WAS fine for both of us. I would think about her sometimes, though. It was hard to not call her when something good happened—I got a promotion at work, for example. I was always torn about calling her if I was going on a business trip. For some reason, it was important to me that she knew that I was going to be out of town. She is my mother, I would remind myself, trying to convince myself to call her. Try not to hate her, I would tell myself.

Sometimes before one of my trips, I would call one of my sisters to see if she knew anything that would give me a reason to get in touch with our mother. I didn't speak often to my sisters. Either one of them. To me, they were the same person with different names, and as we got older, we had less and less in common. I found I had very little to say to them—and they to me. And besides, they reminded me of living with my mother and I really didn't want to think about that.

Sometimes I would just decide I had the right to call her no matter how vicious our last fight was. She was my mother, after all, I would remind myself. It's not like I'm an orphan.

She would always ask me the same question before my trip, whether it was for business or a vacation: How could she get in touch with me if something bad happened?

My answer would always be the same: "Like how bad?"

"Like if someone died," she would say.

I would tell her that if someone died there was really little I could do to help so what would it matter, anyway?

What would I do if *she* were to die? she would ask me.

"While I was on a trip?" I would ask her back. "Or in general?"

You wouldn't care if I died, she would tell me.

"You'll be around for a while," I would tell her. "Don't you worry."

Only the good die young, I would think.

When I returned from my trip, we would settle back into a routine where we spoke once a week, usually on Sunday nights. The time away helped us both. We also knew to not stay on the phone too long. We could be cordial for only a short time.

One Sunday night, a week before my twenty-ninth birthday, she told me she wanted to take me to lunch to celebrate and was even willing to come into Manhattan. I was surprised and pleased. I knew not to invite her to my apartment. She told me to pick the restaurant. "Pick someplace nice," she said. "I want to take you someplace nice."

We agreed to meet at a restaurant that had been written up in the *Times*, across the street from Bloomingdale's. I didn't tell her how I chose the restaurant, and she didn't ask. I don't remember what we talked about, but I remember thinking how nice it was to be with her and wished that it hadn't taken so many years for the two of us to manage to have a nice lunch together and have an adult conversation. At the end of the lunch she told me she had something she wanted to give me for my birthday. She handed me a small plain white box—she didn't wrap it—and I was shocked when I found a pair of pearl earrings with little diamond spokes sitting on a square piece of cotton. Those earrings were my mother's—I think her mother bought them for her after my father died—and she knew I loved them. I always admired them when she wore them. I didn't know what to say. After a few moments I asked her if they were really for me.

She said they were.

"Really?" I said.

"I want you to have them," she said. "I know you love them."

"But why?"

She told me it was because it was my birthday and couldn't she give her daughter a present? And that I shouldn't be so surprised. She was happy that I was doing so well at work and she wanted me to have something that I loved and that I would remember I got from her on my birthday.

I wanted to hug her, but I stopped myself. I didn't want to make her uncomfortable. We never hugged each other. She asked for the check and I asked her if she was sure she wanted to pay. She said she did. I looked at the earrings again and told her I loved them. I still couldn't believe she had given them to me. I closed the box and put it in my small black leather, rectangle-shaped pocketbook that I wore across my chest. I zipped it shut. I saw her get ready to say something, but she stopped.

We walked out of the restaurant and I hailed a cab for her. I wanted to make sure the driver wouldn't give her a hard time about going back over the bridge into Queens. Before she got in, I thanked her again for the earrings and lunch, and kissed her on the cheek. I remember her cheek felt dry and strange to me. I couldn't remember the last time I had kissed her. She didn't kiss me back. She closed the door to the cab, and I waved her off.

It was the middle of winter, but it was a clear, sunny day, and I decided to walk the fifteen or so blocks back to my apartment. On the walk home, I thought about the earrings and my relationship with my mother. I was touched that she wanted me to have them. I was happy that our relationship was changing, and I realized that I wanted to forget all of the things I had hated about her. I realized it didn't matter anymore.

I couldn't wait to get home to try on my new earrings and see how they looked on me in the mirror. I was going out that night and decided I would wear them. I found myself walking quickly, almost running. I got to my apartment building a little out of breath. I walked into the small vestibule that opened into my building—the area where the mailboxes were—and I unzipped my bag and pulled out my key chain. I saw the little white box sitting on the bottom of my bag and I smiled. As I turned the key and pushed open the door, a man came behind me, grabbed my bag, and pulled it away from me. He didn't say a word. I let him pull the bag over my head—I remember bending my head down so that the bag wouldn't hit my face as it went over me—and he ran out the building.

A moment later, I followed him outside. I stood in front of my building and started to scream. I couldn't move. I watched as he ran to the corner and then disappeared around it. I realized I was still screaming. I made myself stop when I saw that there was no one there to hear me. I walked back into the building, opened the door again—thankful that I still had my key in my hand—and then walked up the five flights of stairs to my apartment. I unlocked my door, put my key on the little pink marble table where I ate my breakfast each morning, and with my coat still on, called 911. I was told someone would come to my apartment soon. And then I dialed my mother's number. As soon as she answered, I started to sob. I couldn't stop. I told her what had happened and that I had called the police.

"He took your bag?" she said. "With everything in it?" We both knew what she was asking.

"He took my earrings," I whispered. "He took the earrings you gave me."

She took a deep breath. I wondered if I caught her in the middle of smoking a cigarette.

"I wanted to tell you to put the earrings in your pants pocket," she finally said.

Her words stopped my crying. "You did?" I demanded. "Why didn't you say something when you gave them to me? Why didn't you tell me to put them someplace else when we were in the restaurant?"

"I wanted to," she said. "But I was afraid you would tell me I was being ridiculous. That I was insulting your precious Manhattan. I wanted to tell you to put them in your pocket just in case someone stole your bag. But I didn't think you would listen to me."

The doorbell rang and it was the police.

"I can't talk now," I told her. "I'll call you after the police leave."

We didn't talk about the earrings ever again.

# CHAPTER 21

THE NEXT MORNING SHE called me and asked how I was doing.

I was fine, I told her. I was fine.

The next morning after that, she called me to see how I was doing.

I was still fine.

She would call me as soon as she got into the office and we would chat about anything. The weather. What her boss said. What her mother was going to have for dinner. We spoke about everything and nothing.

A few months later, I met the man I was going to marry.

It was a chance meeting at work. He was looking for an advance copy of that Sunday's *New York Times Magazine*. He had written a piece in it, he told me, and he wanted to see how it turned out. Someone had told him my department always got early copies of the magazine and that I would have extras. I did. We chatted for a while, and I wrote my telephone number on one of the copies I gave him. I told him to call me soon, and he promised he would.

That afternoon, as I walked home with my best friend from work, I told her I had met the man I was going to marry. That I knew this tall, handsome, wonderfully gentle and funny man was the one I was going to spend my life with. She laughed and told me to invite her to the wedding.

I didn't tell my mother about him immediately. I had gotten used to telling her little about my personal life as I didn't want to allow her to hurt me. My relationships were my secrets. She didn't need to know whom I was seeing. But this time was different. This was the man I was going to marry and I couldn't keep him a secret forever. But I worried that she would find something wrong with him—and that I would have to write her out of my life again. Perhaps forever. And I realized I didn't want that.

I shouldn't have worried. My mother loved the guy.

And he loved her back.

I needed to figure out what he saw in her that I didn't.

"She has a great sense of humor," he would tell me all the time. "She's such a New York City street kid, with that accent."

My mother had a mixed Lower East Side and Queens accent. She drank "cawfee" and ate "chawklette." Her accent wasn't as distinct as her mother's, who said "earl" when she meant "oil." But it was still obvious where she came from. It bothered her that I didn't sound like her. She would remind me I was a snob and that I was pretending to be someone else because we didn't speak the same way.

"Who do you think you are?" was her constant refrain.

When my future husband and I first started dating, I had to decide when I was going to introduce him to my mother. I knew that he was close to his mother. I hated admitting I wasn't close to mine.

When I called to tell my mother I was bringing someone home and that he was someone important, she was thrilled. She never believed I would find someone "good enough for me"—according to me, she would say. And she would remind me that I told her I would never settle for just anyone. She once told me she never thought I would get married.

I never thought I would, either.

After my father died, I decided I would marry a man who would rescue me from my mother. When I played with my Barbie and Ken dolls, Ken didn't talk; he just did what Barbie told him to do.

When I was in high school, I had a crush on a boy who had my father's smile and who played basketball. The boy called one day when I wasn't home. My mother told him I would call him back. She never gave me the message.

In college, I dated men who had dark hair and wore beautiful sweaters. I had a fight with my middle sister when the man she was dating didn't open the car door for her. "How could you let him get away with that?" I lectured her. "If you don't expect to be treated well, you won't be," I fumed. She didn't listen. I wouldn't consider dating a man who didn't open doors for me, I told her.

One of my boyfriends had blond hair. I never had a blond boyfriend before. I introduced him to my mother, and she called him the Weasel behind his back. I decided I wouldn't bring him home again. After college, I dated men who never asked me about my family and I never told. I wouldn't think to bring any of them home. I wouldn't know how to explain the housedresses and the smoking and the messy apartment. And I didn't want to.

And then I met my future husband.

I never told him about my childhood with her. I decided he had the right to judge her as she was now—not then. Besides, what did it matter? I found the man of my dreams, and my mother and I were on pretty good terms. Especially since we didn't see each other too often.

Whenever he asked a question about her—what was she like, were we close, did we look alike—I would tell him we were very different, and no, we weren't really that close—you know, that mother-and-daughter thing he wouldn't understand—and that you could probably tell we were related if you *really* looked, but that I didn't think there was a major resemblance. She had blue eyes, after all. And that my childhood was probably like any other—some of it good, some of it not so good. Yes, we grew up in the projects, but we moved out when I was fifteen and I turned out okay, don't you think, and that's why I'm so tough, I would tease. Anyway, who remembers, really? It was a long time ago. And why does it matter now? Yes, my father died when I was eleven, and no, she never even went out on a date after he died. How sad is that, I would shake my head. And then I would change the subject.

She invited us to dinner on a Sunday night. He brought red roses, her favorite. I brought dessert. On the way to her apartment, I told him that growing up we lived on hamburgers and TV dinners, and not to expect a great dinner. My sisters and I loved TV dinners. Every week we would go to the supermarket to buy as many Swanson fried chicken dinners as we could fit into a freezer that always needed defrosting. In the evening, we would set up snack tables in front of the television and wait for the timer to ring to let us know that our dinners were ready. We were always happy when we managed to not burn the chocolate brownie that sometimes used to bubble over into the corn niblets.

My sisters and I spent most of our time together in front of the television, I told him. Hours and hours.

On the days that my mother had to work and we were off from school, my sisters and I would start the day with a glass of milk or whatever juice was in the refrigerator and a toasted Kellogg's Brown Sugar Cinnamon Pop-Tart wrapped in a white paper towel so we wouldn't burn our fingers on the hot pastry. Then we would sit in front of the set and watch one show after the other: *Lucy, Green Acres, Petticoat Junction, The Beverly Hillbillies, The Andy Griffith Show*. We would sing the theme songs to each other and tell whoever was singing the loudest—or messing up the words—to shut up. Lunch would be one of those Swanson dinners and then *Hollywood Squares,*

*Donna Reed, Let's Make a Deal, The Newlywed Game,* and *All My Children.*

The set was on all the time, I told him.

Even when my mother was home, she would tell us to watch TV whenever we were bothering her.

"Go watch TV," she would say, waving us off when she was on the phone with her mother. Or sitting at the kitchen table drinking coffee and smoking a cigarette. Or taking a nap in the bedroom. Or going out to get her hair done on Saturdays.

And so we did.

All the time.

I dreamed about having a color television. My sisters and I begged her to trade in our black-and-white for a new color set.

"You think I'm made of money?" she would scold us. "Go watch TV and shut up."

Every year the four of us would watch *The Wizard of Oz* together. That and *The Ed Sullivan Show* were the two shows we watched together as a family without fail. I dreamed about seeing the movie go from black and white to color. A few days before it was due to be on, my mother and sisters and I passed the local electronics store that advertised it was going to show the entire program on one of its new color sets in the window.

"Look, Ma," I said, as soon as I saw the sign. "We can watch it here. We can see Oz in color!"

"Are you crazy?" she asked me, shaking her head. "You think I'm going to stand in front of a store window to see a goddamn movie?"

"Please, Ma," I begged. My sisters chimed in.

"Please, Ma," we begged. "Please, Ma, please, Ma, please, Ma."

And then she agreed. "Fine," she said. "Fine."

That night, the four of us walked the few blocks to the electronics store. My sisters and I were skipping down the street, we were so excited.

"We're off to see the Wizard," we sang. People in the street smiled at us. We looked so happy.

The four of us stood in front of the window watching the movie, and even though we couldn't hear the sound, we knew what was happening from seeing it so many times.

I couldn't wait to see the transformation from black and white to color. I dreamed about seeing the Emerald City. It had to be the most beautiful place in the world, I thought. I pressed my face up against the glass, waiting for that magical time.

The color changed, and I wanted to dance with the Munchkins and Dorothy.

And then we went home to our own set.

"Sounds like you had an interesting childhood," he said, as we got into the elevator of her building.

"That would be one way to describe it," I told him.

I wondered what kind of meal we would have.

My mother opened the door in a housedress. I could tell that it was new. It was royal blue with big red-and-white-checked pockets. My future husband complimented her on her beautiful blue eyes and her thick, dark hair. He bent over and gave her a hug and a kiss on the cheek. I had forgotten how small she was. I wondered how she felt about a man touching her—even that way—after so many years.

"You know," she said as soon as he finished hugging her, still standing in the doorway, "she'll never get an ulcer, she'll only give one," motioning toward me.

He laughed.

"I don't know what you see in her," she continued, shaking her head.

He laughed, again. "She's sweet," he said. "She's a very sweet person."

"Are we talking about the same person?" she asked.

"Thanks, Ma," I said.

She led us into the apartment, and I was surprised to see a new tablecloth on the table. You could smell the fresh vinyl and I could still see the creases that showed she had only recently taken it out of its package. She had prepared a dinner that was perfect from start to finish. She even had made dessert—a sour cream coffee cake, one of her mother's favorite recipes, not the usual store-bought Entenmann's that she served whenever I came to visit.

After dinner, the three of us walked downstairs to the playground and sat on a bench together watching some of the neighborhood kids play on the swings.

Later, as we were driving home, he asked me why I told him she couldn't cook. That was a great meal, he told me. I wondered why we had never had that kind of meal growing up.

I HAD ALWAYS promised myself I wouldn't have the same kind of marriage my mother had. That no matter what, I would not be with a man who couldn't love me and take care of me the way I needed and wanted to be loved and cared for. I always felt sorry for my mother. After my father died, she died a little bit, too.

When I called a few weeks later to let her know my boyfriend and I had decided to get married, she was thrilled.

He was good, he was Jewish, and he made her laugh. She told me she was impressed I found someone like him.

"I don't know what he sees in you," she told me, talking through the cigarette she swore she had given up. "Does he know what he's getting into with you?"

What would she wear? she wondered aloud. What would she do with her hair?

And then she told me she couldn't wait to walk me down the aisle.

But I didn't want her to walk me down the aisle. Since my father had died so long ago, it never crossed my mind that this would be part of my wedding ceremony—whenever I got married. I wasn't close enough to anyone else in my family that I would ask him to substitute for my father. Had my grandfather been alive, my mother's father, that would have been different. But he wasn't. I was surprised that she thought I would want her to do this. I was surprised that she *wanted* to do what should have been my father's job.

I told her it wasn't going to be that kind of wedding. That it was going to be informal, an outdoor wedding. Not traditional. Maybe I wouldn't even wear a wedding dress, I told her. We were going to pay for it ourselves, I told her. She wouldn't have to worry about it.

And that meant no walking down the aisle. With anyone other than my soon-to-be husband, I told her.

She was shocked. "What will everyone think?"

I told her I didn't care.

"But what will everyone think?" she repeated.

They'll think that I'm thirty years old and it's my wedding and I wanted it to be the kind of wedding that I wanted, I said.

I wondered why I wouldn't let her walk me down the aisle. I tried to convince myself to say yes, but I couldn't. I didn't want to tell her I didn't love her enough to have her do this. And that maybe I didn't even like her.

My future husband told me it was my choice, but I know he thought I was making a mistake.

He doesn't know about my life with her, I told myself. He wouldn't understand.

And I didn't want to tell him.

I couldn't stop thinking about my mother's wedding.

My mother married my father when she was nineteen. And she didn't wear white at her wedding.

I wore a long white dress at my wedding. A beautiful vintage lace dress from the 1950s that didn't need any alterations. My mother got married in 1953. She could have worn a dress like mine. I wondered whether her father walked her down the aisle when she got married. But I never asked. Didn't she know how I felt about her? Didn't I know how she felt about me? Did she think that when she got married, her life would turn out the way it did? I told myself it didn't matter. I didn't care.

"You're selfish," she told me when I wouldn't give in.

"It's *my* wedding," I told her.

IT POURED ON my wedding day. The kind of rain that hit the windshield so fast and so furious that the wipers almost didn't make a difference. We couldn't see out of the window. My fiancé and I spoke very little in the car. I know we were both worried about the weather.

We were driving up to my future in-laws' house, where we were getting married. I had had my hair done early that morning in the city. My hairdresser opened his salon especially for me.

It was hot and humid and I worried that my hair wouldn't make it to Westchester, where they lived, let alone through the ceremony. My hairdresser convinced me to use his favorite hair spray, the kind, he said, that would ensure my hair would stay put no matter what. I thought of my mother as he was waving the pink Aqua Net can over my head back and forth and back and forth.

We drove up to the house, parked the car in the driveway, and I ran into the house with my mother-in-law, who had been waiting for me with an umbrella. I went straight into her bedroom to change. As I was getting dressed, I could hear our guests arriving.

I LOOKED IN the mirror and I thought about my mother and my father and their wedding day. I was going to have a good marriage, I promised myself. I was going to have the kind of marriage that my mother didn't have.

I wanted to see her.

The rabbi told us that all of the guests had arrived.

Except for my mother and two sisters. I knew my youngest sister was driving.

My mother was late for my wedding.

My husband-to-be worried that she and my sisters got lost driving in the rain. That they couldn't find his parents' house.

I reminded him that everyone else used the same printed directions. And they were all here.

We waited.

I thought about beginning without her. I knew she was angry and upset that I wouldn't let her walk me down the aisle. I started to think that perhaps she wouldn't come, that this was going to be how she made it clear to everyone how she really felt about me.

I wasn't wearing a watch. I looked at the clock on my in-laws' dresser. We were supposed to begin twenty minutes ago.

We were waiting in my in-laws' bedroom—the only room in the house that was air-conditioned on the hottest, rainiest day of the year—when someone announced, "She's here."

SHE RUSHED into the bedroom, and standing in my long, white wedding dress, I looked at my mother, whose black eye makeup was streaked in ugly circles under her eyes. I wasn't sure if she was crying or just got caught in the rain.

"You look beautiful," she said to me.

I didn't want to cry.

"We got lost," she said. "We couldn't find the house."

I leaned forward and we patted each other's backs. I had forgotten how small her shoulders were.

"I can't believe how beautiful you look," she said again.

I shook my head. "Don't make me cry," I begged her.

She touched my hair. "You look beautiful," she repeated.

I noticed there was a lot of gray in her hair. I wondered why she hadn't colored her hair for my wedding.

I didn't look at her as my husband and I walked down the aisle together, out in the back lawn, under the tent. But after the rabbi announced we were married and everyone clapped, I saw she was the only one who didn't.

# CHAPTER 22

AFTER I WAS MARRIED, my mother and I settled into a new kind of relationship. We didn't talk about the past—we talked about the now. What my husband and I were doing that weekend. Where we would be going on vacation. What she was having for dinner. Nothing important, but it was civil. And I was glad.

My mother never asked me when I was going to have a baby. I was never one of those women who dreamed of having babies. When I got married, I knew that one day I would wake up and decide I was ready to have a child. Or not. And I convinced myself that if I did decide I wanted a child, I wanted a boy. Not a daughter.

I worried that if I had a daughter I would repeat the same experience I had with my own mother. That I would hate her—and that she would hate me. Or even worse, I would love her and she wouldn't love me back.

So on that day when I woke up and decided I was ready, I was glad my husband said he was ready, too. I told him I wanted a boy. A boy? he said. But I want a girl. I've always wanted a girl.

A boy will be better, I told him. You'll have someone to play with and I'll have someone to take care of me when I'm old. Boys take care of their mothers. Look how you take care of your mother, I reminded him.

When I called to let my mother know I was pregnant, she was thrilled with the idea of being a grandmother. She made jokes about my having a girl and the "payback" I would have with a daughter. "You think it will be easy?" she warned me. "You should hope for a boy," she said.

All throughout my pregnancy, people would stop me—on the street, in restaurants, at the office—and tell me I was having a boy. Because of the way I was carrying. Every time my mother spoke to me she told me I was having a boy. You're better off, she would tell me. Girls are trouble, as you know.

She would call me every Sunday night, right before *60 Minutes*, and remind me that when she was pregnant, she didn't have to wear maternity clothes until her seventh month. That she hardly gained any weight and lost it soon after she had each of her three girls.

I didn't need to wear maternity clothes until my seventh

month. And I lost my pregnancy weight two weeks after I had my own girl.

A girl. A daughter.

When the doctor told us she was a girl, I felt the immediate rush of happiness—and the immediate rush of dread. A girl, I thought. A girl. A daughter who would have everything in common with me and would never fight with me and would love me no matter what.

A daughter who would have nothing in common with me and would fight with me all the time and hate me because I was her mother.

"A girl?" she kept asking when I called to let her know the news. "You had a girl? You didn't have a boy?"

Once my new family was home, my mother would call each night to ask how her granddaughter was doing—and ask when she would see her. When we did go to visit, she would look at my daughter, who would sit and smile in her baby seat, and tell me it wouldn't be like this forever.

I would laugh and tell her that I would be a good mother and that of course it would.

"You'll see," she would tell me. "You'll see."

"You're right," I would tell her. "I will."

I THOUGHT ABOUT my mother a lot when I took care of my daughter. As soon as she would cry, I would pick her up. I carried her with me everywhere. I wanted so much to have a different kind of relationship with my own daughter, and it was going to be different from the very beginning. My daughter was going to love me no matter what, I knew.

I wouldn't raise my voice and I wouldn't make her stand in a corner.

I wouldn't hit her with a strap. I wouldn't call her names.

One morning, I was home with my daughter, just the two of us. I was still on my maternity leave and my husband had left early for work. I hadn't hired a babysitter just yet. My mother called to say hello. She told me she bought my daughter a new doll and that she couldn't wait to give it to her.

As soon as I hung up the phone, the crying began.

It wouldn't stop.

I patted my daughter's back. Her cries got louder. I carried her into the kitchen to warm up her bottle. I hated breast-feeding—I never felt I was feeding her enough—and put her on the bottle as soon as I thought it wouldn't mark me as a bad mother. My mother never breast-fed her daughters. She told me she thought the whole idea was disgusting. And besides, she said, her breasts were too small. She couldn't imagine there would be any milk, anyway. And who did that sort of thing in the 1950s when she had her babies, anyway?

The bottle didn't work.

Her diaper didn't need changing.

Her little face became redder and redder. I started to worry that the neighbors would think that I was hitting her.

There was nothing I could do to stop the crying. I held her as close as I could to my chest—I hoped the beating of my heart would help soothe her.

It didn't help. Maybe my heart was beating too fast.

I tried singing. Her cries got louder.

And then I got angry. I could feel myself getting angry at this person who wouldn't listen to me.

I held her away from my chest and told her to stop. Stop crying, I said. My voice got louder. STOP. CRYING. NOW. I could feel my whole body tensing.

She wouldn't stop.

Her eyes were open but she wasn't looking at me.

I started to walk over to my bed—my arms outstretched holding this baby I didn't recognize—and I had to stop myself from pushing her face down into my pillow. I was shaking.

She wouldn't stop crying.

I could feel myself wanting to take the pillow and put it over her mouth. I just wanted her to stop crying. I could feel myself hating her.

And then I remembered a conversation I had had with my mother when I was around twelve years old. The front page of one of the newspapers on the kitchen table told the story of a mother who had thrown her baby out of the window.

"How could a mother do that?" I asked my mother. I couldn't believe something like that was possible.

She looked at me for a long time and didn't say anything. She took a sip of her coffee and then took a long drag on her cigarette. She twisted her mouth, blowing the smoke out of one side.

"Don't you think that's terrible?" I demanded, waving away the smoke with my hand. "How could a mother do that to her child?" I repeated.

She turned away. "I could understand a mother doing that," she said.

I couldn't believe what I was hearing.

"You're a sick, sick person," I told her. "And you don't deserve to be a mother."

"When you're a mother, you'll understand," she said, still not looking at me. "You'll understand."

I FORGOT WHERE I was for a moment.

And then I realized my daughter had stopped crying. I picked her up and hugged her against my chest.

And then I started to cry.

I never talked with my mother about what it was like for me to grow up with her. I think she knew. And I think she too wanted to forget. My daughter was going to bring the two of us together. For the first time, we would have something we could share. We were both mothers. And one of us was going to be a good one.

# CHAPTER 23

My mother became a different person after my daughter was born.

Or maybe she already was that person. Maybe she just needed my daughter to help show me that other side, the side I never saw growing up.

For once we had something in common—we both thought my daughter was the most important person in each of our lives.

And we had something else in common—we both wanted to have a good relationship with her.

I was especially touched by how gentle my mother would

be when she was around my daughter. And how afraid she was to hold her. She would tell me she couldn't possibly remember how to hold a new baby and that she was afraid she would drop her. And I would remind her she had three babies and that she hadn't dropped any of them, huh, did you? I would tease.

Just sit on the couch, I would tell her. And then I would hand her my daughter.

Every time we got together, she would bring a present. A new book, a new stuffed animal, a new outfit. I would tell her she really didn't need to spend any more money and that we had everything we needed. She never listened.

She would send me money—a hundred dollars here, fifty dollars there—and tell me to "buy something for the baby," or "put it in her college fund." She was insulted when I told her I really didn't need the money, so I stopped telling her that.

I never knew how much money my mother made, and she never talked about how much money she spent. She never talked about her savings. I knew her parents had helped her with her expenses when she was married to my father, and I assumed they continued to do so after my father died.

Sometimes she would give my daughter a piece of jewelry. A little gold bracelet, a necklace with a little gold heart, a ring with an opal—my mother loved opals and knew my daughter would, too.

"Put it away for her," my mother would say after giving me a little white box with a new piece that sat on top of the fluffy white cotton square. "Give it to her when she's older and tell her it was from me."

"You'll tell her yourself when she's big enough to wear these things," I would tell her back.

My mother loved jewelry. After my father died, she turned her engagement ring into a small diamond chip necklace that she rarely wore. It was too small for a ring, she told me when she decided to make it into a necklace. I was horrified that she would destroy her engagement ring. Didn't Daddy give that to you? I asked. Don't you want to remember you were married to him?

She told me she knew it would look better as a necklace. And besides, she admitted, she was always embarrassed that the stone was so small. Especially when her sister had a much bigger ring when *she* got engaged.

Whenever my mother bought a new piece of jewelry for herself, she would hide it in one of her closets, in the pocket of a coat or a jacket she hadn't worn for a while. Sometimes, she would wrap her things in aluminum foil and store them in the freezer or in an empty coffee can in the kitchen. Or in the back of a drawer. Often she would forget where she had hidden different pieces and would spend hours going from drawer to drawer, closet to closet, pocket to pocket, trying to remember where she last put something when she wanted to wear it.

Wouldn't it be easier, I would ask, when she would tell me how upset she was when she couldn't find something, to just keep everything in one place? A jewelry box, perhaps?

You don't understand, she would tell me. I work hard for my money, and I don't want my things to be stolen. "Money doesn't grow on trees, you know," she would say, or, "I don't have the kind of money you have."

Long after I moved out of her house, my mother would always tell me I spent too much money on things that weren't important. You're just like your father, she would tell me.

"You wouldn't be so free with your money if you had to depend on someone else to give it to you," she would lecture me.

"You're right," I would tell her. "And that's why I don't."

That's why, I would remind her, I always worked. I never wanted to ask her for anything.

And then: "But isn't it a mother's job to help her children?"

I knew I was talking about my relationship with her.

And we both knew I wasn't talking about money.

She looked at me. "When a mother can," she replied. "When she can."

MY MOTHER ALWAYS told me how beautiful my daughter was.

"She doesn't look like you did when you were a baby," she would tell me. "You were pretty ugly. I was always so embarrassed when people would look at you and tell me you were cute when I knew you weren't."

"Thanks, Ma." I would laugh. "Thank you for sharing that."

"But you're pretty now," she would say.

Thanks, I would tell her again.

"And smart. You were always smart."

Sometimes she would ask me if I planned to have another child.

I had always wanted to be an only child. "Just one," I would tell her. "Just one child is enough for me."

"She'll be lonely," she would warn me.

"She'll have friends," I would tell her back.

I was thirty-three years old when I had my daughter, ten years older than my mother when she had me. I couldn't imagine having a baby when I was twenty-three. Or twenty-five. Or twenty-six. Just like my mother.

"She'll have friends," I said again.

And then, "You're a good grandmother. Who would have thought?"

She laughed. "Now I have something to live for," she said.

# CHAPTER 24

I DIDN'T TELL MY mother she was going to die.

I couldn't.

I knew she wouldn't have wanted to hear.

I found out my mother was sick after one of our Sunday phone calls, in the fall of 1992. I had been married four years and my daughter was two years old. On this Sunday, my mother called early that morning instead of in the evening. I was surprised when I picked up the phone and heard her voice on the other end.

She hadn't been feeling well lately, she told me, and had gone to an emergency room earlier that week.

She had a lump on her neck and it seemed to be grow-ing. She didn't have a regular doctor, so she went to the emergency room of the hospital not too far from her apart-ment. I think she told me that my youngest sister drove her there. She said she didn't want to bother me. She said she was having a hard time swallowing. They took some tests. I wondered if she had seen a doctor since my youngest sister was born thirty-three years ago. I asked her what the doctor had told her.

My mother said the doctor told her to call for the test re-sults yesterday.

"So what were the results?" I asked.

She didn't answer. I motioned for my husband to lower the volume on the TV.

"Hello? Are you there? What did he say?"

"I didn't call." She could barely get the words out.

"You didn't call? Why not?" I stopped myself. I tried not to raise my voice. I didn't want her to hang up on me. I didn't want to go back to our old relationship.

"I'm afraid to hear." She sounded like a little girl.

I sighed and told her to give me the doctor's name and number. I'll call him, I told her. And you'll see how silly you're being.

"You'll call him?" she said. "You'll call him now?"

Right now, I told her. Assuming he's in. It's Sunday, you know.

"He's in," she told me. "I just checked a few minutes ago. But he'll be leaving soon, so you need to call him now." I didn't ask her how she knew this. I assumed she called, asked if he was there, and then hung up before he could get on the phone.

I told her I would call her back as soon as I reached him.

When I finally got through and identified myself, I asked the doctor if he could tell me what was wrong with my mother.

He said he couldn't tell me anything and that she, the patient, had to call to get this information.

I told him that she wasn't going to call him.

She has to call, he told me. I can't speak to anyone else, he repeated.

She's not going to call you, I insisted. Ever.

I asked him if he wanted to be responsible for her. For whatever happened. And that I could assure him she would never call him, and if he didn't tell me, she was never going to hear about it. And that if he didn't want to be responsible, he needed to tell me what was wrong with her. Please.

The doctor told me he thought she had lung cancer and that he didn't think she had much time. He gave me the name of a pulmonary specialist. He told me she needed to see him immediately.

She had only six weeks to live, he told me. If she was lucky.

From cigarettes? I asked.

From cigarettes, he said.

I started to think about going to eat Chinese food with my mother and father and sisters on Sunday nights when my father was home and not sick. The endless cigarettes they lit up between dishes.

About traveling in the back of the car with the two of them smoking and having to stop by the side of the road because their cigarettes made me sick.

About my mother never seeing my first apartment in Manhattan because I wouldn't let her smoke.

About coming to visit my mother after I moved out and not wearing any of my good clothes, afraid that I would smell like cigarettes.

About her sitting at the kitchen table, smoking. All the time.

I DON'T REMEMBER hanging up the phone. I think I handed it to my husband.

And then I had to tell her.

My husband asked me what I would say. I dialed her number quickly. I didn't want to think about what I was going to say.

She answered on the first ring. "Did you talk to the doctor?" she asked.

"I did."

She didn't ask what he said. I knew she wouldn't.

I told her she was pretty lucky.

The bad news was that she had lung cancer—but that if she was going to get any cancer, this was the one to get. This was the one that was curable. She would be fine. But she would have to see a doctor tomorrow. I already had a name. I was told he was the best. I would meet her at his office.

"What will you do with the baby?" she asked. "Who will take care of her?"

My daughter was just about three years old.

I told her not to worry. That she should meet me at the doctor's office the next morning. We had an appointment at nine A.M. She would be fine, I told her, again. Talk about dodging a bullet, I told her. You really are so lucky, I told her. You got the one that is so easy to cure. I turned away from my husband. I saw the puzzled look on his face and I didn't want to be distracted. I was careful to keep my voice light. I knew she would believe whatever I said. She knew I wouldn't lie to her. I didn't offer to come over. I knew she would know something wasn't right if I told her I was coming over. I called my sisters and told them I was taking her to a doctor tomorrow and that I would call them once I knew more. I didn't give them details. I didn't want either one of them to tell her anything I knew she couldn't hear.

I got to the appointment early and told the doctor I didn't plan to tell her the truth. And to please help me.

He said he couldn't lie to her if she asked.

She's not going to ask, I told him. She's not going to ask.

She didn't ask.

I watched while he examined her. She hadn't put lipstick on that morning. Her lips were cracked and dry. She held a crumpled-up tissue in her fist. She wore little gold stud earrings that looked like little twisted knots. Her light brown loafers were scuffed. She hadn't combed her hair.

She looked like my mother, but I didn't recognize her.

When the doctor told her she would have to have chemo immediately, I worried that losing her hair would kill her before the cancer did. I knew she wouldn't think about dying. Her hair would be what she would think about.

We walked out of the doctor's office and didn't say anything until we got outside.

"I can't do this," she told me. "I just can't."

"Yes, you can," I told her. "Yes, you can."

"I can't lose my hair," she told me.

"Maybe you won't," I told her. "Maybe you'll be one of the lucky ones."

During her first chemo session, I watched as she kept patting her hair while the medicine dripped into her veins. I could see she was relieved—and surprised—when nothing fell out.

After the session, I told her we should go look at wigs. Just in case.

"Do you think I'll lose my hair?" she asked me.

"Let's get one. Just in case."

We went to a little shop on a side street, a few blocks from her doctor.

I was glad there was no one else in the shop.

"We're looking for a wig for her," I told the woman. "Something that looks like her hair now."

"Cancer?" the woman mouthed to me when we both saw she wasn't looking.

I nodded.

"Let me show you some nice styles," she told my mother. "I think I have one that will match your hairstyle."

She handed her the wig and told her to put it on.

My mother shook her head. "I can't," she told us both. "I just can't."

"Yes, you can," I told her. "Put it on and let's see how it looks." I handed it to her.

She picked up the hair and looked at it.

"Let me help you," the woman said. "Let me show you how to put it on."

My mother closed her eyes.

The woman put it on her head and moved it around. She patted it into place.

My mother's eyes were still closed.

"Open your eyes, Ma," I told her. "It looks great. You would never know."

She opened her eyes and looked in the mirror. She nodded her head.

"Will it fall off in the wind?" she asked. "Never mind," she answered herself. "I'll wear a kerchief."

The next time I saw her, her hair looked like it hadn't been washed in weeks. "Why is your hair so greasy?" I asked her. "Is your shower not working?"

She didn't answer.

"Why don't you go to the beauty parlor?" I pushed. "They'll wash your hair for you."

She shook her head. "I'm afraid if they wash it, it will all fall out."

"You don't know that," I told her. "Maybe you'll be one of the lucky ones and it won't."

She looked at me.

"You can't not wash your hair," I told her.

"Maybe tomorrow," she said. "I'll probably do it tomorrow."

"Do it now," I said. "I'll stay with you."

I waited while she went into the bathroom, and I could hear the water running. She came out with her head covered with a towel. She went into her bedroom and closed the door.

I looked in the tub and saw that her hair did fall out, in ugly clumps. I cleaned out the hair with a tissue and threw it into the toilet. I flushed the toilet twice, to make sure it all disappeared.

The next time I saw her, she was wearing the wig. We never talked about her hair again.

# CHAPTER 25

WE NEVER TALKED ABOUT her illness. We never talked about what might happen. Or when.

My mother never asked questions. By this time, I wasn't worried that her doctors would tell her anything. They knew her well enough to know that she wasn't interested in the truth. My sisters and I agreed we would never tell her she was going to die soon. She was going to be fine, we told her.

Her routine never changed.

In the weeks and months following her diagnosis, she would wake up each morning, have her coffee, and drive a few blocks to work. She now worked as a bookkeeper in a local electronics company. She had learned to drive a few years earlier. My middle sister and I used to joke that her world consisted of a five-mile radius—the only distance she would drive her car. Her disease made her world a little bigger.

I would always wonder if she ever thought about smoking a cigarette, and then I got angry at myself for thinking that.

She would call me soon after she arrived in her office. She asked her boss if it was okay to leave early on the days she had to go into Manhattan for her chemo treatments. She scheduled her appointments late in the afternoon so she could do as much work as possible before leaving. I told her she should stay home on those days. Or at least take off the next day to relax. She told me she was fine and that she didn't want to lose her job.

"Besides," she would tell me, "who would do my work if I wasn't there?"

Sometimes I would meet her at her doctor's office and would watch as the drug dripped into her vein. Sometimes one or both of my sisters would be there, too.

My youngest sister had a son three years younger than my daughter, and she kept telling me how much she wanted our mother to be alive for her son's first birthday.

My middle sister had divorced her first husband years before and was now dating a much older man.

My mother would tell her to marry him, that she should have someone to take care of her.

Whenever I visited my mother and my sisters weren't there, she would tell me how important it was to her that the three of us become close. I wasn't close to my sisters growing up and I wasn't close to them now. When my father was alive, I wondered if they really understood what was happening in our parents' marriage. We never talked about it. When my father died, I decided to live in my own world—and I didn't need or want them in it. As far as I was concerned, they couldn't be part of my life if they were part of my mother's. I always wondered what my sisters thought when my mother and I fought. And if they cared. Now that my mother was sick, it was the first time we had a good reason to be together. I realized I really didn't know who they were and I was sure they didn't want to know me, either. They reminded me of everything I wanted to forget. When I lost my father, I lost my sisters to the other side—my mother. And I didn't know how to get them back. I didn't know if I wanted to get them back.

During those times we were alone, my mother and I never talked about what was happening to her. We could chat about my daughter, my husband, my work. My sisters. She always wanted to talk about my sisters. My mother would tell me she couldn't understand why my middle sister wouldn't marry the man she was seeing.

"Convince her to marry him," she would tell me. "This way I won't have to worry about her."

"He's old," I would tell her. "Almost your age. Maybe *you* should date him," I would tease. My mother would blush and change the subject. I knew she never dated a man after my father died.

"Be nice to your youngest sister," she would tell me, wagging her finger at me. "She means well and she wants you to like her. She takes good care of me," she would add. "I couldn't manage without her and she deserves to be treated better by you.

"Take care of your sisters," she would tell me. "That's all I want."

I told her I would try.

We would chat about the weather. What I was wearing. Sometimes she would ask me if I was a good mother.

And then she would answer the question herself.

"You're a good mother. I could see that," she would say.

I would smile.

"I never would have believed it," she would add.

WE NEVER TALKED about her dying. I convinced myself she really didn't know.

I kept trying to forget that the doctor had said she had only six weeks to live. I kept imagining the calendar and tried to forget the date when I had first heard the news. I couldn't believe she would be gone soon.

But then we passed the six-week mark.

I asked the doctor if he thought he might have been wrong.

"She's very, very sick," he told me. "She's not going to last much longer."

"But she's still here," I reminded him. "And you said she would die in six weeks."

I realized that didn't sound the way I meant it.

"You're right," he said, scratching his cheek. "I didn't think she would last this long."

"So maybe you're wrong," I insisted. "What else could it be?"

"Maybe she decided she doesn't want to die," he said.

"She doesn't *know* she's going to die," I shot back.

"Even better," he agreed. "Even better."

THE WEEKS TURNED into months, and there were times I thought she might actually defy the odds. Maybe she wasn't going to die soon, after all. Maybe life would be back to normal soon.

Aside from going to her chemo and then radiation treatments, her life didn't change all that much.

And she looked the same.

I never knew if any of her hair grew back.

She usually wore her wig with her kerchief whenever she left the house or her office. At home she wore one of her many terry cloth turbans. She said they were more comfortable. She told me she wouldn't look in the mirror when she put them on. I wondered if she slept with them.

She insisted on going to her treatments by herself.

And she wouldn't accept any money from me or my sisters to take a taxi or car service.

After she finished work, she would drive her car back to her apartment building, park, and then walk to the corner to take the bus to the subway. When her treatment was finished, she would go back into the subway and then on to the bus home. It usually was rush hour, and she admitted she often didn't get a seat on either.

"Can't you go during lunch or later in the morning?" I

would beg. "And then go to work after that? At least you would get a seat."

"Mind your business," she would tell me.

"And I'm not spending money on a taxi, either," she would add right away. "So don't even bring it up.

"I'm fine," she would tell me. "Just fine."

SOMETIMES I WOULD ask her why she didn't ask her sister—who lived in the building next to hers—if she would drive her there. Or at least pick her up and take her back home after a treatment. At least once in a while.

"I don't want to bother her," my mother told me.

"But she's your sister," I said. "And she goes into Manhattan with her husband almost every day, anyway."

My mother always looked up to her sister.

The two of them were two years apart, but it might have been two hundred.

Growing up, my mother was the good girl and her sister was the one who hung out with the "bad" crowd, my mother used to tell me. "How bad?" I used to ask. Bad enough, she would reply. She would come home at all hours, my mother told me, and would never listen to her mother or father. She smoked and drank and wanted no part of her family.

When they were young, my mother was short and fat with long dark hair. Her sister was tall and skinny and was blond. She always had a cigarette hanging from her mouth, my mother told me.

My mother's sister had lived in Brooklyn after she got married and then moved to the Bronx. When the neighborhood started to change, she bought an apartment in the same co-op development as my mother and moved into the building next to my mother's. I always thought it was strange that the two of them didn't spend a lot of time together.

"She only wants to be with her husband," my mother used to tell me when I would ask. "Two's company, three's a crowd," she would remind me.

"But she's your sister," I would insist.

My mother would shake her head. "You don't understand," she would tell me. "I don't want to bother her," she would add.

One afternoon my mother called me from her office and let me know she had just heard from her sister. She and her husband offered to pick her up after her treatment that day. They couldn't take her there, but they would bring her home. My mother was thrilled.

Later that evening, I called and asked her how she was and told her how glad I was that her sister finally offered to help. And how great it must have been for her to get home quickly and without a hassle, right?

She told me that she had to wait a half hour for them to arrive at the hospital. She thought she had told them when she was supposed to finish, but maybe she gave them the wrong time. That was okay, she said. It wasn't too cold out so it wasn't a big deal waiting for them. She was just a little tired and just wanted to go home and take a nap. She knew they would be here soon. It was so great when their car pulled up, so much better than taking the subway even though—and I mean that—taking the subway was no big deal. Her sister rolled down her window and waved her into the backseat. But when she looked in the back, she saw the seat and the floor were filled with grocery bags. Maybe they didn't realize they were there.

Get in, her sister told her, without getting up or opening the door. Get in now, she said. It's cold out here. My mother waited a moment and her sister motioned for her to get in, telling her to hurry up. My mother opened the door and squeezed into the seat, arranging her legs so that they didn't mess up any of the bags on the floor. She put one of the bags on her lap. Now she had more room. She told me how tired she was and how much she looked forward to getting home quickly. She said it didn't matter that she had the bag on her lap. It wasn't that heavy. She couldn't wait to get home.

But first, her sister told her, they had to make a stop on the Lower East Side—to pick up sneakers for her husband, who was driving. "You don't mind, do you?" she asked my mother, who was sitting in the back of her car, squeezed between her sister's grocery bags. "You can just sit in the car until we finish."

My mother told me she didn't mind.

"You've got to be kidding," I told her. "They couldn't drop you off first and *then* go get his damn sneakers?" I couldn't believe what I was hearing. "And you couldn't tell her you didn't feel well and you wanted to get home?"

I told my mother I was going to call her sister and tell her off. "What kind of person is she?" I demanded. "She's your sister, for chrissakes."

"Don't bother," my mother told me. "It's fine. That's the way she is. She only cares about herself and her husband."

Besides, my mother repeated, she didn't mind.

And that she knew she could never depend on anyone to take care of her. And that I shouldn't either. Except maybe that nice husband of mine, she said. And maybe my daughter. One day. But no one else.

THE WEEKS TURNED into months, and it became clear my mother was starting to get worse. I would try not to notice how thin she was. And how weak. She had trouble breathing, and soon her doctor told her she would be better off in the hospital. At least for a while. She could get her treatments there and she wouldn't have to worry about taking care of herself, my sisters and I told her.

I told my mother at least she wouldn't have to wait for her sister to take her to her chemo or radiation treatments. I was glad when she laughed and told me I was right.

I was at a business meeting out of Manhattan when my mother called my office to let me know she was going back into the hospital. She left a message telling me she didn't know what was wrong, but she was having a hard time breathing and swallowing. She would call me when she was checked into a room.

When she couldn't get me on the phone, she tried my husband in his office and he agreed to meet her at the hospital. "Meet me at the emergency room," she instructed. "That's where I have to go first."

He told me that by the time he got there, she was already inside and on a stretcher, waiting for one of the doctors to see her and check her in. She kept complaining that her hip hurt and that it hadn't started hurting until she got to the emergency room.

"I'm falling apart," she told him.

"Don't worry, Ma," he said. "We'll fix you up and get you out of here in no time."

She kept complaining about her hip and she kept patting the area on the stretcher. She reached under the blanket and found a syringe.

"Oh, my God," she said to him. "Look what I found that was sticking me."

She handed the syringe to my husband.

"What if I get AIDS?" she asked. "What if I get infected with something?"

He looked at her.

And then she looked at him and said, "I guess that would be the least of my problems, huh?"

And then she laughed.

THE NEXT AFTERNOON I stopped by and saw her alone in her room. My sisters and I took turns visiting during the work-week, and my middle sister was expected soon.

She wasn't sleeping. She wasn't reading a magazine. She wasn't watching TV.

Her bed had been cranked up so that she was somewhat sitting. I wondered how long she had been awake. She spent more and more time sleeping when we came to see her. The morphine, her doctor told me, was kicking in.

A few days before, her doctor told me that she was failing fast and that he didn't think she had much more time. Really.

And this time I could see for myself he was right. You can see how sick she is, he told me. And that he would be happy to give her more morphine so that she wouldn't be in pain.

"Is she in a lot of pain?" I asked.

"She could be," he said. "She never complains. She told one of the nurses she doesn't want to bother anyone."

My mother never wanted to bother anyone.

"But the morphine will help," he said.

"She needs it," he told me.

"It's going to be soon," he told me. "You need to get ready."

"Just don't tell her anything," I reminded him again. "Don't tell her she's going to die."

She was looking at the wall when I came in. I could hear her breathing and could tell she was having a hard time.

She turned to me when I came in. "You look nice," she told me. "You always look nice."

No, she didn't need anything.

We sat together, saying nothing.

I couldn't stand the silence.

I asked her if she was in pain and she told me, no, she had this little button she could press whenever she was. She pressed it a lot, she told me.

"You know," she said, "your father lived on this stuff."

I didn't know what to say.

She continued. "He was an addict, you know. He couldn't live without his precious morphine."

I didn't know.

"He used to shoot himself up all the time," she told me. "Every day when he was home."

And then I knew.

She turned away from me. She continued.

"His doctor gave him morphine to ease his pain," she said. "His physical pain," she added.

And then she closed her eyes.

"I promised myself I would never take this drug," she whispered. She shook her head. "And here I am. But now I know why he liked it so much."

And then I remembered finding him in the kitchen with the needle in his thigh.

The trips to the drugstore.

The white paper bag.

His doctor kept telling him it would make him feel better, she told me.

"And now I'm living on it, too," she said. She shook her head, again. "Funny how things turn out."

I didn't know what to say.

I was glad my middle sister came into the room. I didn't want to have this conversation anymore.

The three of us chatted about the weather and my mother complimented my sister's coat.

Then a doctor I had never seen before came into the room.

He was tall, very tall, well over six feet, and large. You could tell he couldn't button his white coat and that's why he kept it open. He smelled like coffee. He wore thick brown glasses that kept slipping down his nose. He kept pushing them back. He grabbed her chart and the three of us watched while he read it. He glanced over it and spoke to my mother directly.

He asked if these two beautiful young ladies were her daughters.

My mother nodded.

He looked like he was my age. Thirty-seven.

"I just looked over your chart," he told her. Yes, we could see that.

She nodded, again.

"And I think you know," he continued, "that we've done everything we can to help you."

He patted her leg under the blanket as he was talking.

"I wish we could do more," he told her, as he was patting her leg.

Stop patting her leg, I wanted to tell him. Stop talking, I kept thinking. And who the hell are you, anyway? I've never seen you before, so get out of her room. Now.

"I wish we could do more," he said, still patting.

Stop talking, I kept thinking. Stop, stop, stop. Don't you know you're not supposed to say anything?

"I wish we could do more," he said again. "But there's really no hope. There's just no hope."

My mother looked like someone had just told her she was going to die.

My middle sister sat in her chair with her mouth open.

I sat in mine thinking, oh, God, oh, God, what am I going to do now?

The ticker tape in my head kept going around and around. He's ruining everything, I thought. She wasn't supposed to know she was going to die. No one was supposed to tell her. Who is this asshole, anyway? What am I going to do what am I going to do what am I going to do?

I finally heard words come out of my mouth. "Excuse me, Doctor," I heard myself say. Anything to stop him from patting her leg. And talking.

He looked up.

"Thank you," I said. "I think we can take it from here."

He stopped patting her leg. Finally.

"Thank you, again," I said. And then he left.

The three of us looked at each other. It was very quiet. We heard the whirring of my mother's oxygen machine. She looked very old. I noticed her eyes were no longer blue, not even light blue. She kept looking at me. Her hands were resting on top of the blanket. They didn't move. She wasn't wearing any jewelry, not even the gold knot earrings she always wore. She looked so small.

I stood up and told the two of them I would be right back. My mother asked where I was going. My sister said nothing. I told my mother I would be right back and to just wait and not get up. And then I realized how stupid that sounded. I'll be right back, I told them again.

I left the room and headed to the nurses' station a few feet away. The doctor who had just told my mother she was going to die was surrounded by some of the pretty nurses who would come to my mother's room every day to see how she was doing. And to make sure the morphine button was working. And whatever else she needed. She never really needed anything else. She really hated bothering anyone.

I walked right up to him and looked up. His glasses slipped down when he looked down at me and he pushed them up.

"Excuse me," I said, not caring that I was interrupting his conversation. "Excuse me. Can you talk to me for a moment?"

The nurses were still surrounding him.

"Excuse me," I said again, not wanting to raise my voice. I didn't want my mother or sister to hear what I was saying. "I need to speak to you. Now."

I could smell the coffee on his breath.

"Do you know what you just did?" I lectured him. I shook my hand at him, pointing my index finger at his chest.

"Do you know that we have been hiding the fact that she's going to die from her? Did you know that? Did you know that? Do you know that's maybe why she's still alive? Did you know she was supposed to die in six weeks and it's now almost a year and a half later? Did you know that? And you come in and then you take it all away? In a moment? Didn't you take a goddamn Hippocratic oath? First do no harm? Isn't that what they teach you? And who the hell are you, anyway? Who told you to say anything? How could you ruin this for us? How could you do this?"

I was shaking. I didn't want to cry. The nurses were quiet.

The big doctor looked down at me. "I'm sorry," he said, meaning it. "I'm so sorry."

"How could you do that?" I repeated. "How could you?"

"I'm sorry," he said again. "I didn't know. What can I do?"

I thought about my mother thinking she was going to die.

"You can go back," I said. "In five minutes. Not a minute more. And you can tell her you made a mistake. That you just realized it sounded like you were telling her she was going to die and that there was no hope. That you just meant she couldn't get any more chemo now and that she would be scheduled in a few months or so." I didn't stop for breath.

Later I learned that as soon as I left the room, my mother sent my sister out to see where I was going. My sister told her she didn't know what I was saying, but that I was waving my hand a lot at the doctor.

He looked at me and said he would do this.

Thank you, I told him. Thank you.

I took a deep breath, turned around, and went back into her room. My mother and sister looked at me as soon as I came into the doorway.

I sat down.

"It's too good," I said when I sat down. "It's too good."

My sister asked me what happened.

"It's too good," I repeated. "But I don't want to ruin it."

"Ruin what?" my sister said. My mother didn't say a word. She just stared at me.

"Just wait," I said. "Wait. I think there's been a big mistake, but I don't want to ruin it."

The three of us waited, saying nothing. I tried not to glance at my watch.

In five minutes, the doctor reentered the room and stood where he stood before. He didn't pat my mother's leg.

I am so sorry, he told my mother, sounding like he meant it. I am so sorry, he repeated. Your daughter just explained to me what you thought I said and I am so sorry. I wasn't saying you were going to die now, he said, I just meant we can't give you any more treatments until you're a little bit stronger, but I expect that will be soon. And then in a few months, we'll give you another round of chemo and after that, it should do the trick. Again, he said, shaking his head, I am so sorry if I scared you. I didn't mean it.

And then he left.

And then my mother said, "Oh, thank God. I thought he was telling me I was going to die!"

And then I realized I didn't want her to die. That I wanted her to live. And that I wanted to start all over.

# CHAPTER 26

I GOT THE CALL on a Monday afternoon just as I was getting ready to leave my office.

"You need to come now," the home nurse told me. "She's not doing well."

My mother hadn't been doing well for a long time. The cancer that was supposed to kill her in six weeks still hadn't gotten her one and a half years later. But lately the disease was on a winning streak and it was clear there would be no more rushes to the emergency room. There was no more hope, her doctor had told me again. And this time I believed him. He told me there was nothing more they could do for her in the hospital. It was better, he told me, if she went home. She would be more comfortable there. He wouldn't say how much longer she had, but we both knew it was going to be soon.

But I was convinced she was going to make it to her sixtieth birthday on April 18, only thirty-six days away.

I read somewhere—probably in the *Times*—that women who are on the verge of death will wait to die until the week *following* their birthdays and that most men will die shortly *before* theirs. I had hoped this would be the one time she would get her way.

I thought about this as I raced down the street, knowing I would have to fight with the cabdriver to take me to Queens from Manhattan during rush hour. And I was tired. Of fighting. Of everything.

I found a cab quickly and told the driver that my mother was dying and that if he didn't take me to Queens she would die alone and it would be his fault. He looked at me, paused, and then turned on his meter. Twenty-five minutes later I was ringing the doorbell to her apartment.

The nurse opened the door immediately.

"She's dead," she told me. "It's too late. You should go in and see her."

"She's dead?" I asked. "Was she dead when you called? Why didn't you tell me?"

She just looked at me. It was the first time I could remember her actually saying nothing when I came to visit.

I kept my coat on and walked to the kitchen table. I could see the old cigarette burns on the orange and yellow vinyl tablecloth. I sat down, opened my pocketbook, and searched for the number of the funeral chapel.

"Aren't you going to see her?" the nurse asked.

"I have to call the funeral home first," I said, reaching for the phone.

"But don't you want to see her?"

I put the phone down and looked at her carefully. I thought about my mother and what she looked like before—before the chemo, before she lost her hair, the way she looked in a photo when she was thirty years old and my father was thirty-one and he wasn't sick and none of us were fighting. I thought how we finally had something in common when my own daughter was born three years ago. I thought how sad it would be for my daughter to not remember her grandmother.

I got up and walked toward her bedroom. I realized I was still wearing my coat. I didn't take it off. Her door was closed—I assumed the nurse had closed it after she saw that her patient was dead. I put my hand on the knob and paused. My head was filled with all of the things I wished could have been and all of the things I wished I could have said.

I took my hand off the knob and walked back into the kitchen. This wasn't the way I wanted to remember her.

"Aren't you glad you saw her?" the nurse chirped when I returned. "Didn't it feel good to see her one more time?"

I didn't answer. I just looked at the calendar on the wall.

# CHAPTER 27

THE DAY AFTER MY mother died, my sisters and I met at the funeral chapel to pick out her coffin. We agreed that the funeral would happen the day after next. We didn't care about Jewish law. We weren't ready. We had already agreed it would be in Manhattan and not in Queens. It didn't matter that my mother lived in Queens. None of us wanted to go back there for a funeral. We didn't argue during lunch. I don't remember who paid the bill but I remember we didn't fight about that, either.

After lunch, I took a taxi to one of my favorite stores to buy a new black suit. My entire wardrobe was black, but I decided I had to have a new suit for her funeral. I told the salesperson

I needed the alterations done quickly, that I had to have them that next morning for an event the day after. He laughed and asked me if I was going to a funeral. He didn't laugh when I said yes. I felt sorry for him.

The day of her funeral, my daughter was sleeping when we left to go to the chapel. I had asked my babysitter to come early that day. I told my sitter that my mother had died and to please not tell my daughter. I wanted to tell her myself.

When I got to the chapel, my sisters were already there. The rabbi asked me if I wanted to see my mother in the coffin. Something about Jewish law and making sure we were burying the right person. I couldn't do this. I didn't want to see my mother this way.

The rabbi asked us to describe the kind of person she was.

My husband spoke first.

"She was a real New York City kid," my husband said. "She had a great sense of humor. Real fast with the comebacks. I loved her accent," he continued. "And she was so generous. She loved her records, but if I liked one, she would give it to me. Wouldn't take no for an answer. And she drank a lot of coffee." He laughed.

I just looked at him.

The rabbi turned to the three of us.

Tell me what it was like growing up with her, he asked. What kind of mother was she?

My middle sister told him she was a great mother. That she would do anything for her children.

My youngest sister said she was a great mother. That she would do anything for her children.

I was quiet.

No one asked me questions like these at my father's funeral.

Later, my husband asked me why my relationship with my mother was so different from that of my sisters.

They had a different mother, I told him. They didn't see what I saw, they didn't know what I knew, I tried to explain to him. She treated me differently than she treated them. I wasn't sure he understood. I wasn't sure I did, either.

During the service, I thought about my mother coming late to my wedding. She wanted to walk me down the aisle and I wouldn't let her. I thought about my daughter and how she would grow up. I thought about what would happen to her if I were to die.

My mother's mother sobbed the entire time during the funeral. "No one should ever have to bury their daughter," she kept repeating. No one could comfort her.

My grandmother loved my mother so much. I wished I could have loved her, too.

I didn't talk to my mother's sister at her funeral. I couldn't stop thinking about my aunt living in the building next door to my mother while she was sick and not volunteering to take her to the doctor or to her chemo treatments. Save for that one time.

I thought about no one talking to me at my father's funeral. Had I done something to deserve that? Had my mother?

When we returned home from the cemetery, my daughter was playing with her toys in the living room. I thanked my sitter again for coming early and told her I didn't need her to stay any longer. That I was going to be home now.

As soon as the sitter left, I sat my daughter on my lap and told her that something sad had happened, that my mother had died because she had a disease. But that it was a disease that only old people got. I had spoken to her nursery school teacher a few weeks before when it was clear my mother wouldn't be around much longer. I wanted to know what to say to my daughter. I didn't want to say the wrong thing. Her teacher had told me that as a three-year-old, my daughter would be most concerned about me, and that I had to reassure her that I wouldn't die, too. I kept thinking about how I found out about my father's death. I kept thinking about my sisters running in the hallway singing that our father was dead. Years later, my mother told me she had asked our doctor what she should say to us when my father died. She told me she was worried about how to handle the news when it happened.

"She's dead?" she said. "Grandma's dead?"

"Yes."

"She won't come back?

"No."

"Are you sad?" she asked.

"Yes."

It was at that moment when I realized I really was.

"I'll be okay," I told her.

I'll be okay, I told myself.

I willed myself not to cry.

My daughter looked at me.

"I'll be okay," I repeated.

That night, when I was putting her to bed, I kissed her good night and told her to have sweet dreams. She kissed me back. And then she said, "Say, 'Goodnight, *Mom.*'"

I asked her why I should say that.

She reminded me I had lost my mother and that now *she* was going to be my mom.

I hugged her. I couldn't talk. So I hugged her again.

LATER THAT NIGHT, I sat at my kitchen table drinking a cup of coffee. I walked over to the phone and called my mother's number at her apartment. The phone rang and rang. I was annoyed that the answering machine wasn't picking up. I forgot that it was broken. My husband asked me who I was calling, and when I told him, he looked at me like I was crazy.

"You're calling your mother?"

I shrugged.

"Did you think she was going to answer the phone?" he said.

I couldn't answer.

I could see he was worried that I might be losing my mind.

"She's dead, you know." His voice was gentle.

"I'm not crazy," I told him. "I'm really not."

I know he wanted to believe me. I knew he was thinking about what happened the week before she died, when he and I were walking near Grand Central Terminal together, after lunch.

"Ma?" I called out. "Ma!"

"Who are you talking to?" he said.

"That woman looked like my mother," I tried to explain.

"Your mother's at home in bed," he told me. He shook his head. "How could you think that was your mother?"

"It looked just like her," I told him. It did. It really did.

"But she's dying," he said. "She can barely breathe. Did you think she got out of bed, and decided to go take a trip to Grand Central?"

I didn't know what to say.

# PART THREE

# CHAPTER 28

THE DAY AFTER HER best friend's sweet sixteen party, my fifteen-year-old daughter learned what it's like to lose a parent.

You would think that with all my experience—my father died when I was eleven and my mother when I was thirty-seven—I would be someone who could comfort her and explain why things happen and why some things can't be explained. But I was sitting in the living room at my computer and my daughter was sitting in her bedroom at hers, after having asked me to leave her room because "you don't understand anything about death."

My daughter loves me and loathes me. And while I

shouldn't have been surprised, I didn't like it. I never wanted it to be that way.

The night before, she had gone with four girls to celebrate her best friend's sixteenth birthday with dinner, a limo driving around Manhattan, and then back to another one of the girls' houses for a sleepover. As always, and the rule, I received calls throughout the night keeping me posted: "I'm at the restaurant now." Click. "We're in the car just driving around." Click. And finally, "We're at her apartment." That was at twelve forty-five A.M.—fifteen minutes after her curfew—but it was a sweet sixteen celebration so I didn't say anything. I was happy finally to be able to go to sleep.

At one-thirty, the phone rang again. This time the sophisticated fake grown-up voice reverted back to the fifteen-year-old child. Crying, I heard a word I hadn't heard for years: "Mommy." As in, "Mommy, something terrible happened. My friend's father hit his head in a restaurant and he's in a coma and they think he's going to die."

How do you explain to a fifteen-year-old about death and how it chooses its victims? The next day she and her friends stayed with their friend at her apartment while the girl's mother was at the hospital. I was proud of my daughter and told her that.

"Yeah, whatever," she said.

"They think it's hopeless," she told me.

"Maybe they'll be wrong," I said.

"You don't understand," was her reply. Then I was asked to leave her room.

I tried to hug her, and she let me in for a moment. "You

don't understand," she said again. And then the child in me responded with, "I lost my father when I was eleven. How could you think I don't understand?"

"But were you the favorite?" she asked. I wished one of us would realize this conversation was ridiculous and that one of us should be the grown-up and end it now.

"Absolutely," I said.

"He's going to die," she said. "There's no hope."

MY DAUGHTER AND I had a big fight the morning of her friend's father's funeral.

"Are you going to the funeral?" she asked, expecting me to say, "Of course," since I knew her friend's mother slightly from work and once the four of us went to lunch together.

I didn't have any friends at my father's funeral.

"I have a meeting I have to attend," I told her.

"A meeting is more important?" I could hear the sneer in her voice.

"Don't lecture me," I told her. "She's your friend, not mine."

"You don't understand about death," she told me again.

"You're right," I said. "I wouldn't understand what it's like to lose a parent."

THE CHAPEL WAS filled with hundreds of mourners. I saw my daughter and her friends in the first few rows.

I sat in the back row.

At the end of the service, I saw my daughter with her friends. They circled the girl whose father had died. I didn't have any friends at my father's funeral. I started to walk down the aisle to say hello to them and then changed my mind. I don't know why I didn't want to see her. Was it because I didn't want her to see that I had been crying? I knew she wouldn't understand why I would cry for someone I didn't know. I didn't want to tell her I couldn't stop thinking about my own father's funeral and how lonely I felt.

I hurried out of the chapel and took a taxi back to my office. She never knew I was there.

# CHAPTER 29

THAT WEEKEND, I THOUGHT a lot about the funeral and about my daughter. I thought about my mother and my father and decided that now was the time to open the box—the wooden box with the padlock and the skull and crossbones that my father had given to my mother when they were in high school. The box that had been hiding in my closet all these years. The treasure chest my mother promised me and I had taken from my mother's apartment after she died.

I was going to open it with my daughter.

Maybe my mother was the same age as my daughter when my father gave it to her, I thought.

I had always worried that I would have the same relationship with my daughter that I had with my mother. I never wanted to have that same kind of relationship.

I walked into my daughter's room with the box on a Saturday afternoon, a few days after her friend's father's funeral. She was going through a sixties music phase, discovering the same music I used to listen to late at night when my parents fought. The music that I hoped would help drown out the sounds of the end of a marriage.

My daughter told me she was impressed I knew the words to almost every pop song recorded during that time. "When did you have time to listen?" she asked.

At night, I said. All night long, I thought to myself.

I told her I loved listening to the radio. She didn't need to know the truth, I told myself. I don't know if I'll ever be ready to tell her the truth.

She looked at the box.

"What's that?" she asked.

I told her it was my mother's and that I had been holding it since she died, waiting for a time to open it. The right time. I thought it would be fun for the two of us to open it together.

She looked at me. "Your mother died when I was about three, right?" she said.

"Right."

"I'm fifteen now."

"Right."

"That box has been sitting here for twelve years and you never opened it?" she asked.

I nodded.

"You're weird," she said.

"Yeah, I guess I am," I said.

She invited me to sit on her bed.

"Really?" she asked.

"Really," I answered. "I really didn't open it."

"What were you waiting for?" she asked. Still not quite believing me, I know.

And then I knew this is what I was waiting for.

"For this," I said. "To open it with you."

She seemed pleased.

"You wouldn't have appreciated it until now."

She seemed convinced.

We looked at each other and smiled. I was glad I waited for this moment.

"Are you nervous?" she said.

I was.

"I'll be right back," I told her. I went into the kitchen, looking in the tool drawer for a screwdriver. I used it to pry open the lock.

I flipped open the top. We were both quiet.

# CHAPTER 30

I DON'T KNOW WHAT I expected to find in the box. But as soon as I opened it, I knew the contents would change everything about how I felt about my mother and her life. And I was ready.

The box was filled with letters, about three dozen. Letters to my mother from my father starting when he was sixteen and she was fifteen. Letters he had written to her while she was at sleepaway camp one summer. And when he was in the army a year later.

I pulled out a few from the top of the pile and began reading them aloud to my daughter, one by one.

*My dearest darling,* so many began.

She was loved.

He had told her how much he cared for her and missed her.

> *I miss you, I miss you so much that I am going crazy.*
> *Not seeing you is like not feeling the rain when it*
> *falls, the sun when it rises, nor the moon when it sets.*
> *You are my life, I live for you.*

And how much he wanted to be with her.

> *My dear, I had a dream about you last night. I dreamt*
> *we were married and had six kids and I was a mil-*
> *lionaire and we were very happy together. I hope*
> *that dream comes, though I don't care about being a*
> *millionaire. I'm a millionaire as long as I have you.*
> *You are worth more to me than all the money in the*
> *world.*

My daughter sat on the bed and listened. I asked if she wanted to read a few, too. I handed them to her, but she gave them right back. "I can't read his handwriting," she said. "Keep reading," she told me.

> *Please promise me that we will never, never fight*
> *again, because if we had another fight I'm afraid I*
> *would have a heart attack and die. Because without*
> *you, what good is my life?*

From these letters I learned about his constant colds, the flu, the frequent stays in the army hospital. About the penicillin shots he told her they would give him, to get him back to work.

About how his colds got him kicked out of the *toughest school in this man's army,* as he described the dental technician classes he was taking. The job that was going to make him the money he always wanted and thought he deserved. *They didn't get me out of the hospital fast enough,* he complained to my mother. And then he added, *Don't tell my mother.*

*Are you getting high marks in school?* he asked her. *I hope so as I always said you were the brains in the family.*

I learned that he didn't graduate from high school. And about his smoking.

*I smoke, so what,* he wrote. And he sounded like he was angry. *Everybody smokes.*

"Your father smoked, too?" my daughter asks. She sounds shocked.

He did, I tell her.

"It sounds like he was the one who smoked first. Do you think your mother smoked because of him?" she asks.

I nod my head.

"Maybe," I tell her. "Maybe."

My mother was loved.

> *I love to see your lovely blue eyes light up, and for you to give me a tender kiss. Every night when I go to sleep I take your picture out of my hat and put it*

*beneath my pillow. That's how much I love you. And*
*when I get up in the morning the very first thing I do*
*is take your picture and kiss it tenderly, and say to it*
*good morning, darling. Did you have a good night's*
*sleep? I miss you so.*

He was so jealous of her. He begged her to please not do
anything that would come between the two of them.

*I wish we were old enough to get married, so I*
*wouldn't have to worry about you.*

He told her that he understood she might be lonely. But to
please wait for him to come back if she could.

*I trust you very much, but you know how it is when*
*you are away from a girl. You start to worry.*

And that there would never be anyone else but her for
him.

*May God strike me dead if I as much as looked at an-*
*other girl. You're the only one I care for, and will keep*
*caring for. I know that for sure.*

He told her to go out with other boys so she'd be sure he
was the one. He didn't need to do the same, though, he wrote,
since he knew she was the one for him. He was relieved when
he heard back from her telling him she'd never be with anyone else.

I think about the woman with the big blond hair in his hospital room, the woman with the pink lipstick on her teeth. I wonder if my mother knew about her. And then I realize, of *course* she did. Of course.

And so did I.

I WONDER HOW my mother felt when he broke his promise.

She never broke hers.

YOUR EVER LOVING *boyfriend,* he ended each letter. And then this postscript on one:

> *May you live to be 100 years. May I live to be a 100 years, less one day, so that I may never know you passed away.*

He didn't live to be one hundred, and neither did she. But he never had to live a day without her. He almost got his wish.

"Wow," MY DAUGHTER says. "It sounds like they had an amazing marriage. I hope I have that same kind of marriage."

I don't answer.

"We'll read more later, okay?" I asked my daughter as I put the few letters I read back on top. There were photos beneath the rest of the letters. I didn't feel like reading any more.

"Okay," she said. "But don't go through the box without me. I want to look at the photos, too."

I promised I wouldn't.

THAT NIGHT, AFTER my husband and daughter went to bed, I took the box into the kitchen. I didn't want to break my promise to my daughter. I decided I wouldn't look at the photos, but I took out the letters and spread them on the table.

I wanted to read them all, but first I was going to put them in chronological order. I wanted to read them in the order my mother received them—from August 1948 when she was at sleepaway camp in Mountainville, New Jersey, and he was writing from his apartment on the Lower East Side, to letters that seemed to come almost daily when he was in the army—first when he arrived at Fort Dix, in New Jersey in July 1949 to a postcard announcing he had just arrived at Fort Sam Houston in Texas in October 1949. There were times when he didn't write, and I assumed he was home on leave then. The last envelope was postmarked April 17, 1951. Except it was empty. The return address was torn off, but I could make out the words "New York" written in blue ink by my father. I wondered what he would have written her while in New York—and why there was no letter.

I wondered what my mother thought when she got these letters. And how she responded to him.

> I can't tell you how much I would like to have you in my arms. I'm always happier when I'm with you. You have that extra something that makes me very happy. I miss your beautiful blue eyes, your most gracious smile, your most tender lips, and your most heavenly body and your most divine hair.

I was glad I was reading these by myself. I didn't know if I would share this one with my daughter.

Or the next one:

> *Boy, I got the biggest scare in my life when I received that letter. I thought it was about you know what, and boy was I glad to read it wasn't.*

And then this one, soon after he arrived at Fort Dix:

> *You may have to marry me, because I hate the army. I'm sick and disgusted of it and I'm sorry I ever joined. And the only way I can get out is by marrying someone because if you get married you got to support your wife and no one can live on $50 a month, so the army has to release you with an honorable discharge. If you love me like you say you do, you will marry me. No matter what you decide, my love for you will never, never change because I love you more than anything else in the world.*

He tells her about all of the Dear John letters the guys in his barracks get. The letters that broke so many hearts.

> *It's a shame, that's why I'm the luckiest guy in the world.*

His last letter tells her that he's madly in love with her and can't wait to hold her in his arms. And then he ends with a P.S.:

*God-dammit, make sure you answer this letter with a*
*air mail stamp.*

"Air mail stamp" is underlined over and over in red ink.

I FINISHED READING the letters and started thinking about my mother and father and their life together.

They were two kids who got married too young and who thought their lives would be different. Most of their fights started because he doubted her—and maybe she doubted him, too. My parents fought about everything: money, his health, her parents, his friends—even before they were married. It was almost as if their lives were destined for hurt and disappointment.

The mother and father I knew were the people in these letters. I just didn't know it at the time. Maybe the father I adored wasn't the person I thought he was. And maybe my mother wasn't the person I thought she was, either.

I put the letters back in the box and went to bed.

The next morning, my daughter asked if we could look at the photos together.

"You didn't look at them already, did you?" she asked. I assured her I hadn't looked at the photos.

I took the letters out of the box and reached inside for the photos. There was a photo of my father's ninth-grade class in 1948. Photos of my father and mother. Some together, some apart. She's with the girls; he's with the guys. They looked so old, my daughter said. They were young, I told her. They just dressed older in those days.

We look at a picture of my father. I don't know how old he is. He's wearing a light winter coat. Double-breasted. Maybe tan, maybe gray—it's hard to tell because it's a black-and-white photo. And a dark, striped, narrow tie against a crisp white shirt. You can tell his shoes were shined. The break in his pants is perfect. His hands are clasped in front of him, and he's smiling. I remember that smile. His chin is sharp—he has my jawline and the jawline my daughter inherited. My daughter says he has a triangular-shaped face. Handsome in kind of a boyish way, she says. Innocent and vulnerable, she says. She is surprised he looks so much younger than my mother. "Was she older than him?" she asks. He was a year older, I tell her.

In the box, beneath the photos, were two dinner menus he sent her—one from Thanksgiving and the other from Christmas in Fort Sam Houston. And then I saw there were more letters. But this time, they weren't from him to her. They were the letters I had written to her. When I was at sleepaway camp. Notes and postcards from my trips abroad when I was in college and after. Anything I had written her, she saved in the box. I had always wondered what had happened to my high school report cards—and there they were.

My daughter was impressed. I was astonished.

It was at that moment that I wished I could tell my mother I was sorry. For everything. And that I understood. That it didn't matter anymore.

I hugged my daughter.

I was my mother's daughter.

# EPILOGUE

My husband's father died in 2005 and was to be buried in the same cemetery where my parents were.

It was a cold, rainy day in late November. It was so cold and rainy that the rabbi convinced us to have the service in the cemetery office and not at the graveside. "I'll do a short prayer at the graveside," he promised us. "It will be better if we stay inside." He didn't need to ask us twice.

The rabbi put the torn black ribbon on my husband's sweater. When it's for a parent, the rabbi told us, you put it on the left, next to the heart. I remembered my mother's funeral. I couldn't remember where I had put that black ribbon.

After the office ceremony, we drove the short distance to the place where my father-in-law's casket would be lowered into the ground. The rain was now coming down sideways. I didn't notice the hole immediately. I saw my mother's and my father's headstones a few feet away from where my father-in-law would be. I hadn't realized when we bought the cemetery plots for my husband's parents that they would be so close to my parents.

I hadn't been to the cemetery since my mother had died. It was strange to see their headstones next to each other. They were both the same shape, like a three-dimensional book—the Book of Life, I learned they were called—and both had similar inscriptions:

"Dear Mother, devoted daughter and sister," my mother's read. "Grandmother. And wife."

"Dear Father, beloved husband, devoted father, dear son and brother." He died too young to be a grandfather.

All of a sudden, I noticed that both of my parents had died in March.

And then I remembered that their wedding anniversary was in March.

I wanted to tell someone, but I knew that no one would care. They weren't here for me.

I looked at my parents, lying together next to each other, for eternity. I hoped they were finally happy together. I thought about my mother and how as a child I couldn't understand her anger and hate. How she felt about my father when he was alive—and after he died. What I saw and what I didn't know. And how she lashed out at me. I thought about her marriage and how as a child I couldn't understand how two people could be so unhappy together. I thought about my own life and my husband and daughter. I had a good life. I had a great, supportive husband, a beautiful daughter. I had everything I needed and wanted and didn't have to depend on anyone for anything. Whatever had happened between the two of us throughout the years, my mother had to have had an influence on my life now. That I wanted more than she had and was willing to get for herself had to have played a role in my own happy life.

And for that I was grateful.

And then I wept.

# ACKNOWLEDGMENTS

Where do I begin?

Thank you to Lorraine Shanley, one of my dearest and most generous friends, who believed in my work from the start and supported me throughout. I couldn't have done it without you. Thank you to Robin Straus, my fabulous agent, who took me under her wing and guided me from the moment we met. Your encouragement, your smart and perceptive editing suggestions, and your unwavering interest meant the world to me.

Thank you to my fantastic editor and publisher, Mark Gompertz, who was right about everything. *Everything*. I am so grateful to you for your feedback, your editing, your enthusiasm, your support—and most important, your friendship.

To the other wonderful people at Touchstone Fireside/ Simon & Schuster—most especially the amazing Lauren Spiegel, the brilliant designers Cherlynne Li and Joy O'Meara; and to Marcia Burch, Marie Florio, and Martha Schwartz. Also, thank you to Amber Husbands, and everyone behind the scenes. I couldn't have asked for a better house, and I couldn't be prouder to be an S&S author.

To Jenny Frost and Shaye Areheart—you were there in the earliest stages and inspired me to write more. Thank you. To Susan Kamil and Elizabeth Beier—you have no idea how much your interest meant to me.

To my fellow aspiring memoirists in Nancy Kelton's Tuesday night class—you liked my stories, and that's where it all began.

To Amy Selwyn, Jeff Honea, Mirta Ojito, Deb Shriver, Kate White, John Searles, and Joyce Newman—my early readers and supporters. You were so generous on so many levels.

To Pat Eisemann and Marian Brown—I hope you know how grateful I am. To Esmeralda Santiago—thank you so much for your careful reading and insightful suggestions.

To Frank McCourt, my literary idol—you are my inspiration, and your encouragement will never be forgotten.

To my extraordinary husband, Marc, who believed in me every moment—and made sure I didn't wander too far from my computer every weekend. And without whom I would not have a finished manuscript. Your editing and judgment were invaluable—and you were usually right even when I hated to admit it.

And to Olivia—for being so proud of me. I am so proud of you, too.

Finally, to memoir readers everywhere. You're the reason I wrote this book. I hope you liked it. And I hope it inspires you to write your own story. I can't wait to read it.

*Who Do You Think You Are?*

## For Discussion

1. What is the significance of the book's title, *Who Do You Think You Are?* How does the author answer this question? If asked, how do you think her mother would respond?

2. "Here's how you'll get her back, he told me. I looked at him, not understanding how that diary would help me. Write it down, he said" (page 43). Do you think keeping a journal helped the author work through her anger or just allowed her to keep track of her mother's faults? What purpose do you think journal writing has in our culture?

3. Why do you think the author's parents fought so much? How does Alyse's age and perspective affect our understanding of her parents' relationship? Do you think Alyse is a fair narrator when it comes to describing her

parents' relationship or the relationship she has with her mother? Why or why not?

4. At her father's funeral, her mother gave Alyse her father's favorite necklace. Considering the origin of the necklace, what kind of gesture was this? How did this make you feel about Alyse's mother? What does it mean to Alyse?

5. Why do you think no one offered to drive Alyse's family home after her cousin's bar mitzvah? Who or what was responsible for the tension between the families? Did you think it was strange?

6. How do you think Alyse's relationship with her mother ultimately influenced her relationships in general? And later, how did Alyse's husband's relationship with her mother—and her mother's relationship with him—change how Alyse felt about her?

7. What event prompted Alyse to move out of her mother's apartment for good? Do you think the author or her mother was at fault? Explain your answer.

8. "For some reason, the mere mention of the *New York Times* triggered her anger toward me, long after I moved out of her apartment. Sometimes it seemed as if the *Times* was in some way the cause of our problems" (page 155). Why do you think Alyse's job upset her mother so much? Was there any career choice that would not have made her mother feel threatened? If so, which one?

9. Why did Alyse's mother give her the pearl earrings? Was

she proud of her daughter or finally becoming comfortable with their relationship? How did the theft of the earrings affect the original gesture?

10. Was her mother deliberately late for Alyse's wedding or did she get lost? What do you think the author believes? After the couple was pronounced man and wife, everyone clapped except her mother. How do you interpret that behavior?

11. How do you feel about the author's lying to her mother about her true medical prognosis? When do you think it is okay to lie to a person to protect her? If ever.

12. "My daughter was going to bring the two of us together. For the first time, we would have something we could share. We were both mothers. And one of us was going to be a good one" (page 182). Discuss the theme of motherhood in this book. In what ways is it shown to be both damaging and healing? In the end, how would you describe the relationship between Alyse and her mother? And, finally, would you call Alyse's mother a bad mother? Explain your answer.

13. "That box would give me the answers to my questions: Who were my parents really? And why did my mother end up with so very little in her life?" (page 4). What answers, if any, did the contents of the box give the author? What did you think was going to be hidden in that box? Do the contents of the box change the way you think about her mother? Why or why not?

# A Conversation with Alyse Myers

**In writing this memoir, did you make peace with your mother? If she had the chance to write about her side of the story, what do you think the theme of her book would be?**

I made peace with my mother after I had my own daughter—it was the first time my mother and I really had something in common. I saw how she was with my daughter and realized she could have been a better mother to me— and probably wanted to be—but that the circumstances and stresses of her life got in her way. As I write toward the end of the book, I wished we could have started all over. But by then it was too late.

I think the theme of her book would be "I did the best I could." My mother was handed a tough life—and for whatever reason she just didn't know how to use her difficulties as an impetus to do better. In many ways, she gave up. On everything. I wish I knew then what I know now.

**How long did you work on this memoir? How do you think each of your parents would have reacted to the publication of this book? How would they feel about how they are portrayed?**

I've been writing this book in my head since I was sixteen years old. I took a memoir writing class a few years ago to see if what I had in my head would work on paper. I spent a summer during the weekends while my daughter was on a teen tour writing the first hundred pages—and then finished the rest over the next few months.

I would not have been able to write this book if either of my parents were still alive. It would have been seen by each of them as the ultimate betrayal. We were not the kind of family that spoke about our feelings. We were very much a behind-the-closed-door family. In a funny way, I also think the two of them would have been surprised to know that I knew and saw so much. And how it affected me.

You always think you know your parents—but what I learned is that you really don't. You don't know them when you're a child and you don't really know them when you're an adult. I was fortunate to be left with a gift after my mother died—for me, the ultimate treasure chest—that allowed me to see more of who she was.

**Your mother always asked you, "Why do you want more?" Why do you think you wanted more out of life?**
I was a huge reader as a child—often consuming a book a night (I'm a very fast reader). I also spent a lot of time in the library. As a result, I was a student of other people's lives and could see there was more out there than what I had growing up in Queens. I knew I didn't want to have the same life as my mother—and was going to do whatever I could to ensure that not be the case.

**Your father gave you a diary to write down your feelings, but your mother threw it away before you left home for good. How were you able to remember all the specifics**

**of your childhood and relationships without the diary? Have you encouraged your own daughter to keep a journal? If so, do you worry that she writes about the differences and disagreements you share?**

There are some events that I have relived in my head throughout my life and I can remember them like they were yesterday. The details are as vivid now as they were then. I've done my best to present my story as best as I can remember it. I hope I got it more right than not.

My daughter has been writing in a journal since she was in the seventh grade—I love that! I am sure there are things she has written about me that aren't pleasant—things that I would rather she didn't remember or commit to paper. That said, she has the right to remember the moments in her life, and I would rather be in them than not—no matter how painful they might be to read years later. I've worked hard to have a good relationship with my daughter, and I love her more than she'll ever know. I especially love her confidence and her independence. When she was born, I promised myself I would do all that I could to have a better relationship with her than I had with my mother. Hopefully, when she's my age, she'll remember more of the good than the bad. And know that I did the best I could.

**Even though you hated the fact that your parents smoked and that your mother died of lung cancer, did you ever try smoking? Or was not smoking a way to rebel against your mother?**

When I was about twelve years old, I stole two cigarettes and a matchbook from my mother's purse and went into the bathroom when she was at work and my sisters were at a friend's house. I wanted to see how I looked smoking. I lit the match on the first try and was quite pleased with myself. I took a drag—and as I looked at myself in the mirror, I coughed like crazy and saw that I looked like an idiot. I threw the cigarette, the match, and the second cigarette into the toilet and flushed. I never smoked again.

**You used to do the ironing for your mother at night—a peaceful time when it was just the two of you. Have you carried on that ritual with your daughter? What, if anything, does your daughter remember about your mother?**

I loved ironing—and was quite good at it! But I really don't do all that much ironing anymore and haven't yet taught my daughter how to iron. I'm not sure she wants to learn! My daughter was three years old when my mother died. She tells me she remembers very little about her—save the breathing tube in my mother's nose when we visited her at her apartment just before she died. And maybe her blue eyes— although she admits she might remember that because of what I've told her. As I write in the book, I feel sad that my daughter remembers so little about my mother.

**Education was your escape from a poor and difficult family life. What do you do today to inspire others who are dissatisfied with their lives? What advice would**

**you give to those feeling trapped in a dysfunctional family?**

I've always found reading to be a great way to retreat from life's stresses and noise. Reading used to take me away from my day-to-day life growing up. I was often lonely—and books were my companions. I learned through books to believe that anything is possible—because it is.

The best advice I can give to anyone who feels trapped in a dysfunctional family is to find something you're passionate about—and focus on it until everything else is blocked out. Also, surround yourself with smart and loving people. If you don't have them at home, you must find them outside in order to stay positive about yourself and the future. I worked hard to create the life I wanted, and I wouldn't give up. I also did my best not to let my mother know how much she bothered me—that was my protection, too.

**Your mother used to say, "like father, like daughter." Now knowing what you do about their relationship, do you still see that comment as criticism, or has it taken on a new meaning? What good qualities do you think you inherited from your mother and father?**

It was definitely criticism—my mother grew to detest my father. Knowing more about his relationship with my mother has helped me better understand why she was so angry with him. And she wasn't wrong. I just wish I knew more then. Perhaps inadvertently my mother's experience taught me never to settle—to always want more. I so wanted to have a different kind of life than the one she offered me. In her own way, she forced me to be very independent.

My father loved to be around people and he used writing as an important form of self-expression. I'm grateful that both those traits passed to me. And while he couldn't afford much of what he had or wanted, he did teach me to appreciate good things.

**Suppose your mother could ask you today, in a thoughtful and interested tone, "Who do you think you are?" How would you respond to her now as an adult and mother?**

I would tell her I'm a loving mother and a loving wife and that I'm successful at the things that really matter: love and relationships. I would tell her that she inspired me to be the best mother and wife I can be—and that I'm sorry we didn't have the time to repair the past and learn from each of our mistakes. I would tell her that she didn't deserve to have such an unhappy life—and that I wished it could have been different for her. And that I wish I could have been more of a comfort to her—instead of a thorn in her side.

I would tell her that the fact that I have an incredible daughter and husband must have had something to do with her. I would also tell her I am the luckiest person in the world. And I would thank her for that.